THE CONCISE GUIDE SERIES

a concise guide to

Pastoral Planning

Dr. William L. Pickett

Kevin E. McKenna, Series Editor

ave maria press **AmP** notre dame, indiana

THE CONCISE GUIDE SERIES

The Concise Guide Series, edited by Kevin McKenna, tackles questions of central importance for contemporary Catholicism. Each book in the series carefully outlines the issues, references the necessary documents, and sketches answers to pressing pastoral questions.

Founded in 1865, Ave Maria Press is a ministry of the Indiana Province of Holy Cross.

www.avemariapress.com

ISBN-10: 1-59471-135-6   ISBN-13: 978-1-59471-135-0

Cover and text design by John Carson.

Printed and bound in the United States of America.

Library of Congress Cataloging-in-Publication Data
Pickett, William L.
  A concise guide to pastoral planning / William L. Pickett.
     p. cm.
  Includes bibliographical references and index.
  ISBN-13: 978-1-59471-135-0 (pbk. : alk. paper)
  ISBN-10: 1-59471-135-6 (pbk. : alk. paper)
  1. Church management. 2. Theology, Practical. 3. Pastoral theology. I. Title.

  BV652.P53 2007
  254'.02--dc22

                    2007027067

For Matthew H. Clark
Bishop, Friend, and Fellow Disciple

CONTENTS

Preface   11

1. Introduction to Pastoral Planning   15

What Is Pastoral Planning?   16
   Process
   Praying
   Thinking
   Together
   Acting
   Being the Body of Christ
   In a Particular Time and Place
   Summary
What Does it Mean to be a Vibrant Faith Community?   23
   Faith Community as a Communion
   Baptism and Eucharist at the Center
   Diversity
   Response to Change
   Study and Learning
   Liturgy, Preaching, and Prayer
   Beatitudes in Action
   Union with the Larger Church
   Joyfulness
   Summary
What Is the Work and Character of Effective Pastoral
   Councils?   31
   Member Characteristics
   Relationship to the Pastor
   Authority

Collaboration
Summary
An Overview of Pastoral Planning at Three Levels   36
  Diocesan
  Parish / Faith Community
  Intermediary or Regional Groupings
Conclusion   40
Study Questions   41

2. Pastoral Planning Basics   43

Important Planning Considerations   44
  Effective Planning Requires a Process.
  Planning Is About Change.
  Effective Planning Is Based on Agreement About the
    Present.
  "No One Of Us Is as Smart as All of Us."
  Quality Is More Important Than Quantity.
  Two Kinds of Planning: Directive and Probablistic.
Implications for Pastoral Planning   50
Key Areas of Pastoral Concern   52
  Word
  Worship
  Community
  Service
  Temporalities
Characteristics of Effective Pastoral Planning   55
  Comprehensive
  Sufficient Resources
  Involvement of Those Affected
  Effective Leadership
  Prayer and Faith Sharing

Conclusion   58
Study Questions   59

3. Basic Elements of a Pastoral Plan   61

Mission Statement   62
Vision Statement   65
Goals   71
Objectives   73
Annual Action Steps   74
Involvement of Major Groups in Key Planning Elements   75
Pastoral Leader
   Pastoral Council
   Planning Team
   Faith Community
   Staff
   Ministry Leaders
Conclusion   81
Study Questions   84

4. The Pastoral Planning Cycle   85

The Mission Statement   86
   Reviewing an Existing Mission Statement
   Revising an Existing Mission Statement
   Creating a New Mission Statement
The Vision Statement   94
Assessing Where We Are / Gathering Information   95
   Internal Demographics
   External Demographics
   Evaluating Key Areas of Pastoral Concern
   Assessing Guidelines and Constraints

Looking at Other Sources

Focusing Information 102

Identifying Concerns, Issues, and Ideals 104

Engaging the Faith Community 105

Revising and Finalizing Issues & Opportunities 106

Developing Goals 108

Articulating Objectives and Action Plans 108

Engaging the Faith Community 111

Implementing and Assessing 111

Conclusion 112

Study Questions 112

5. Implementation at the Parish Level 113

Organizational Issues 114

   Parish Pastoral Council

   Pastoral Planning Team

Path Forward 118

Parish Pastoral Planning Process 121

Conclusion 144

Study Questions 145

6. Implementation at the Diocesan Level 147

Organizational Issues 148

Path Forward 149

Focus 150

Diversity 152

Ownership of the Process 153

Prayer 154

Diocesan Pastoral Planning Process 154

Special Relationships 165

Diocesan Bishop
Diocesan Finance Council
Priests' Council
Diocesan Staff
Diocesan Pastoral Council
Three Special Issues 170
Strategic Planning
Special Projects
Staffing for Planning
Conclusion 173
Study Questions 174

7. Implementation at the Regional Level   175

Formation of Regional Groups 176
Creation of Regional Pastoral Councils 179
Role of Diocesan Staff 182
Path Forward 186
Clearly Stating the Need for Planning
Criteria, Guidelines, Policies
Projecting Key Planning Variables
Making Resources Readily Available
Connecting with Other Regional Councils
Deadlines and Expectations
Configuration Planning 192
Regional Pastoral Planning 211
Conclusion 213
Study Questions 216

8. Communication   217

What Is Communication? 218
The Basics of Communication 221

During Times of Change, It Is Impossible to
    Overcommunicate.
Repetition Is the Heart of Effective Communication.
Provide Small Bites Rather Than the Whole Steak.
Opportunistic Communication Can Support a Formal
    Communication Process.
Informal Communication Has a Disproportionate
    Impact on Receivers.
People Are Not at Their Best When They Are Surprised.
The Truth Will Set Us Free, Even if the Truth is
    Troublesome.
Feedback That Makes a Difference is Crucial.

Techniques For Listening   226
  Active Listening
  Focus Groups
  Listening Sessions
  Surveys
  Unsolicited Input

Communication Plan   233
  Key Audiences
  Key Messages
  Media

Implementation   237
Conclusion   238
Study Questions   241

Appendix A: Resources   243
Appendix B: Glossary   248

This book is based on my more than forty years of experience in administration and planning in not-for-profit organizations. The first thirty years I worked almost exclusively in Catholic higher education; the last nine were spent as director of pastoral planning for the Catholic Diocese of Rochester, New York. When I began working for the diocese, I brought a great deal of experience in planning: what worked, what didn't, and some notions of why. For several years I had taught a course in leadership as part of an MBA program and always saw leadership as focused on change and thus inevitably on planning.

I was not nearly as familiar with the "pastoral" part of pastoral planning. I had been a committed and involved Catholic for my entire life. I had worked for church related colleges and universities. I had a sense that the Catholic Church that changed as a result of Vatican II was a better church than the one in which I was formed, but frankly, I had little understanding of the theology of Church and practically no experience in the workings of a diocese. Like most lay people, I had a very hazy idea of what the diocesan administration looked like and had trouble keeping offices and their relationships straight.

Fortunately, I began doing pastoral planning in a diocese that was and always had been firmly committed to the ideals of Vatican II and especially to the role of the laity in the Church. I was formed in a Vatican II ecclesiology by my professional colleagues, both within the Diocese of Rochester and in other dioceses, by the Bishop and Vicar Generals for whom I worked, by the pastoral leaders of the parishes and faith communities of the diocese, and, most powerfully, by the lay people of the diocese who took their role in the

Church seriously and worked through many challenges and difficulties in realizing their commitment to the Church.

Toward the end of my nine years of service, I began a Master of Arts degree in theology at St. Bernard's School of Theology & Ministry in Rochester. These courses helped me to gain a fuller understanding of my experience of the Church and to reflect on that experience in light of tradition and scripture. These courses also provided me with a vocabulary to describe my experience in ways that would prove helpful in the work itself and in the writing of this book. Although I am not sure I intended it this way, this has been a process of "faith seeking understanding."

When Fr. Kevin McKenna, General Editor of the Concise Guide Series, approached me about writing this book, I saw it as an opportunity to integrate much of the writing I had already done, both in my role as director of pastoral planning and in the several presentations in the workshops and conventions of the Conference for Pastoral Planning and Council Development. Early on I realized that simply piecing together these existing texts would not provide the coherence and perspective needed. As a result, I began anew to think and write in a comprehensive way about pastoral planning into which I integrated, at particular points, the fruits of my earlier reflections.

Pastoral planning takes place at three different levels in the Catholic Church in the United States: parish, diocesan, and regional. Each level has its own issues and challenges and yet all three need to fit together harmoniously. My first issue was to determine a basic approach that would include all three levels. I decided to develop a generic model of pastoral planning and then apply it to each of the three levels. This results in some unavoidable overlapping but provides the most comprehensive view of the subject and does so in a way that makes clear that the same basic process is used in all three.

Chapters 1–4 develop this generic approach to pastoral planning. Chapters 5–7 apply that model to each of the three levels. Chapter 8 deals with communication as a separate topic. All involved in pastoral planning at any level agree that effective communication is the key to an effective process. Regardless of the technical details of a planning process, accurate and effective communication is essential to planning that has any chance of garnering the support and commitment of those who will implement the plan and those who are impacted by it. Missing this crucial step has scuttled many otherwise well-conceived plans.

Many people have contributed to my understanding of pastoral planning. Bishop Matthew Clark, to whom this book is dedicated, gave me the opportunity to work on behalf of the community of disciples of Jesus Christ called the Diocese of Rochester. I was formed in important ways by his friendship and personal example as well as by his understanding of the pastoral exercise of authority. No matter how I might feel about a situation, I knew that I was always there as one representing him and that I needed to exercise my authority in a way compatible with his understanding.

My colleagues at the Diocese of Rochester gently and sometimes not so gently nudged me in the right directions. I worked for two Vicars General, Joseph Hart and John Mulligan, and served with an extraordinary group of professional colleagues as diocesan directors. I worked directly with a talented team in pastoral planning: Casey Lopata, Karen Rinefierd, Deb Housel, Richard McCorry, and Mary Ann Fackelman. Each, at different times and in different ways, helped me come to understand what pastoral planning was all about. Mary Moorhouse, our administrative assistant, ably assisted all of us.

I was active in the national professional organization for pastoral planning, the Conference for Pastoral Planning and Conference Development, and was privileged to serve on the board of directors for three years and for two years as chair. My colleagues on that board helped me gain a wider perspective about the work of pastoral planning and the role of pastoral councils.

Finally there were colleagues and others who read the manuscript and made many suggestions to strengthen and clarify it. I am truly grateful for their labor of love. They include Fr. Kevin McKenna, Casey Lopata, Karen Rinefierd, Deb Housel, Maria Rodgers-O'Rourke, Richard McCorry, and Erin Pickett-Kessler, my youngest child and mother of two of my eighteen grandchildren. The text has also benefited from the careful attention of Eileen Ponder of Ave Maria Press. In the end, of course, the text is mine including any errors, misstatements, and lack of clarity.

Finally I want to thank my wife, Marilyn, who lovingly supported me even when I disappeared into the study at all hours of the day and night to meet rigorous deadlines. I am blessed to have her in my life and to be in hers.

CHAPTER 1

Introduction to Pastoral Planning

Every effective organization recognizes that change is a constant and that adaptation to change is essential to its continuing life and fruitfulness. As a result, every effective organization plans its future. In its simplest terms, planning is the process of being clear about the present, projecting a future that seems desirable, and specifying the steps necessary to arrive at that future. Is pastoral planning simply this kind of planning done by a faith community or a religious organization?

The answer is yes and no. Yes, in the sense that there is much about pastoral planning that is similar to planning in every organization. In fact, if a faith community is not engaged in planning of this sort, it will not thrive and possibly not even survive. The answer is also no, in the sense that pastoral planning adds new dimensions and proceeds in ways very different from those of planning done in other organizations.

This chapter begins with a definition of pastoral planning. We will discuss the key elements of this definition to help us better understand pastoral planning and the ways in which it differs from planning in other organizations. After that, we will deal with the question of vitality: What makes a parish vital, and why is it essential to answer that question? Next we will review the nature of pastoral councils and their role in pastoral planning. Finally we conclude with a brief overview of three levels of pastoral planning: diocesan, parish and regional.

What is Pastoral Planning?

Pastoral planning is the process of praying and thinking together about the actions of the Body of Christ in a particular time and place. This deceptively simple sentence contains the fundamental notions of pastoral planning and how it differs from other types of planning. The first difference we might notice is the language itself. This is not the language of organizational analysis and planning. We are entering a world that is different from our ordinary experience of human organizations. It is a world that makes sense only in light of the incarnation, life, death, and resurrection of Jesus Christ—God become fully human.

A discussion of each element in our definition of pastoral planning will help us come to a deeper understanding of what it is and the ways in which it differs from other types of planning.

PROCESS

Pastoral planning is a process, a coherent set of activities with internal consistency and identifiable goals and outcomes. Since groups of human beings engage in these activities, there are discernable roles and relationships among them. Pastoral planning is not simply *an* activity but a purposeful *set* of activities that should make the best use of our human understanding about effective group action.

Because it is a process, pastoral planning has a beginning, middle, and an end. As a result, we should be able to locate ourselves in the map of the process. However, because it is a process, it is constantly changing. Ironically, we need to plan because our world constantly changes, and the process we use for this planning is itself subject to this very same flux. Nevertheless, we will see in the next chapter that it is always essential that we have a plan to plan—an initial path forward—even though we know we will likely need to change it.

PRAYING

The most detectable difference between ordinary planning and pastoral planning is the central role of prayer and faith sharing. A group doing pastoral planning is centered in prayer. This has an impact on the nature of the human interactions among group members, as well as the way in which each member approaches tasks and issues. However, this impact does not occur simply because a group begins each meeting with a prayer, as good as that practice certainly is. Too often such prayers become rote, something to be gotten out of the way at the beginning of the meeting so the real work can commence.

The prayer that changes us—and our relationships—is much more profound and, frankly, takes more time. The work of pastoral planning is the work of the Holy Spirit done through and with us. It requires openness on our part to the work of the Spirit in us and in each other. While recited prayers—especially those with which all are familiar—are important, they should prepare us for a scripture-based faith sharing in which we are called to reflect on the ways in which God is and has been present in our lives and to share those stories with the other members of the planning team. It is in telling our stories of the ways in which God has been in our lives and in hearing those stories from others that we are opened to the Spirit working in us and in others.

THINKING

Pastoral planning is both praying and thinking. One without the other is deficient. While prayer opens us to the actions of God in others and ourselves, human wisdom and applied social science provide us the methods to discover, design, and implement concerted human actions on behalf of our mission. A group that only thinks—that is, uses only human understanding—finds it difficult to deal with the truly pastoral. A group that only prays but avoids using the best techniques of applied social science finds itself frustrated and bogged down in the predictable problems of group interaction and decision-making. Effective pastoral planning must be truly incarnational: fully spiritual and fully temporal. Obviously, we must be astute in our use of applied social science. It is always possible that some techniques imported from the secular world may unintentionally undercut some of our important values about reality and human nature. We must be vigilant in our choices but never simply reject any technique developed in a secular environment.

TOGETHER

Perhaps nothing is more characteristic of pastoral planning than its collaborative nature. This is planning that we do together based on the gifts with which we have been blessed and the needs of the faith community. Pastoral planning is collaborative in the radical sense identified by Loughlan Sofield and Carroll Juliano (See **Collaboration** in Appendix A). True collaboration is based on a complete and radical dependence on the gifts of all members of the faith community. This dependence takes the form of a radical identification, release, and uniting of all the community's gifts in service to the mission of the faith community.

Pastoral planning is not something that a few people with greater status, power, and authority do to the rest of us. No matter how wise, correct, and elegant such plans might be, they are at odds with the fundamental understanding of a faith community and the Body of Christ. Pastoral planning that is done by authorities and presented to the "faithful" nearly always raises the issue of the way in which the plans were developed. Once this issue is raised, the content of the plan recedes in importance, and energy is devoted to determining who is in charge—who has the right to tell the rest of us what to do. In addition, if we have no sense of involvement in the planning, we will develop little ownership of the resulting plan and little interest in implementing it.

While we all have different roles in the faith community, we must all live by the admonition of Jesus that our leaders—those in formal positions of organizational authority—not lord it over us but rather serve us (Mt 20:25). Leaders in a Christian faith community must be devoted to creating human systems that include all and empower all so that results truly reflect the fullness of the Spirit present in the community. We must all be and see others as companions on the journey animated by a radical faith in the presence and guidance of the Spirit.

ACTING

As is true of all planning, pastoral planning must be focused on changes in behavior. In the end, the praying and thinking together must result in actions taken in the world to advance the kingdom, the mission of the faith community. Documents, pastoral letters, mission statements, prayer cards, rallies, and celebrations are all important to a Catholic faith community, but without actions they are, as Paul said of words without love, like a "noisy gong or clanging cymbal" (1 Cor 13:1). They make no real difference in the world, the world we are called to bring into the Reign of God.

Actions are measurable; they exist in the external world of human endeavor. Because they are measurable, there is the persistent danger that our planning proceeds too quickly to actions without understanding the relationship between actions and the praying and working together from which they arise. It is a natural tendency for us to take action in order to reduce our discomfort in the face of uncertainty. A set of actions, no matter how well described and organized, does not bear fruit without the thinking and praying process. At the same time, simply praying and thinking together without the development of concrete, specific, and measurable actions allows us only to live in a world of delusion and illusion. The Spirit works to the fullest in time and space, not the theoretical or abstract world of good intentions and great ideas.

Our incarnational sacramentality helps us live in this ambiguity without falling prey to the temptation of focusing on one or the other. Actions without prayers and prayers without actions fall short of the fullness of life that the Lord promised us. We must live with a foot in both worlds, steeped in the knowledge that the Spirit is with us always.

BEING THE BODY OF CHRIST

We are the Body of Christ. Jesus is present in the world through our presence in the world, doing the work to which he calls us: announcing the good news of the Reign of God. As disciples we are called to step away from the values and dynamics of the world in order to enter into the world of the Spirit, the world of the new and fuller life to which Jesus calls us. As we enter this new life, we do the work of Jesus by announcing the good news to all, particularly to those whom the world has discarded and devalued, all those on the margins. We live our lives in a way that proclaims that reality.

Pastoral planning is not about building up the faith community as an institution, but rather about building up a body that constitutes the ongoing incarnation of the eternal God into our world of human achievement and suffering. Unlike secular institutions, which are focused on their own survival and growth, the Body of Christ is a communion of all those who have entered into the mystery of the death and resurrection of Jesus. This is a communion that takes as its motto, "those who lose their lives will find them" (Mt 10:39). A central and undeniable part of the mystery of salvation in Jesus Christ is that we enter into our own ongoing death and resurrection and thereby continually—and once and for all at the end of our lives—enter into the fullness of the Paschal Mystery and into the divine life of the Trinity.

Unlike a secular institution that seeks at all costs to avoid failure and impossible dreams, the Church sees them within the context of its mission and the Paschal Mystery of Jesus Christ. The criteria by which we judge the vibrancy and vitality of the Body of Christ cannot be simply the same measures of success that we use to assess the vitality of secular human organizations.

IN A PARTICULAR TIME AND PLACE

Further, the fact that we are the Body of Christ means that each of us, as faithful followers of Jesus, constitutes a person, alive and vital in the world as it is right now. The one thing we know about bodies is that they change both in themselves and in their adaptation to the world around them. If they do not change, they die. We have the promise of the Incarnate God that the Body of Christ will not die.

Thus it, too, must change and adapt while maintaining its fundamental reality.

The circumstances confronting a faith community in twenty-first-century America are totally different from those that confronted a faith community in first-century Palestine. The circumstances in Boston, Massachusetts, are different from those in Orange County, California, and different from those in Iraq or Australia. The precise look and feel of a faith community in each of these places and at each of these times will be different and, indeed, must be different if the Body of Christ is to deal with the world as it really is. Jesus was an itinerant preacher who was formed in his spirituality through tradition, his relationship with his Abba God, his contemplation, and his interaction with those whom he encountered on his journey. He learned about himself and the world and was able to integrate that with his religious and spiritual life and thus express the life and love of God in ways that were powerful and potent. "He spoke with authority" (Lk 4:32).

Pastoral planning is designed to help our faith communities have the same radical connection to the here and now and to live the spirituality of our tradition, scriptures, and ongoing relationship with God just as Jesus did. Our pastoral planning must be done in a way that results in actions of the Body that are powerful and potent in announcing the Reign of God to the world as it is.

SUMMARY

Pastoral planning is the process of praying and thinking together about the actions of the Body of Christ in a specific time and place. As we have seen, pastoral planning is not a technical organizational function that we use from time to time. It is an essential element of our response to the call to be disciples of Jesus Christ. We typically live out this call in communion with other disciples. It is to the vitality of these communities that we now turn.

What Does It Mean To Be a Vibrant Faith Community?

Pastoral planning often faces the question of the vitality or vibrancy of a parish. This usually comes up in a discussion of which parishes might or should be closed. After all, so the argument goes, we can only afford to have vital parishes; we cannot waste precious resources—especially priests—on parishes that score low on some index of vitality. So the question of what constitutes a vital or vibrant parish is of more than passing interest. Indeed, the vitality of a parish is a fundamental issue for pastoral planning. If pastoral planning does not focus squarely on creating, sustaining, and increasing the vitality and vibrancy of specific faith communities, it focuses on the wrong things. To think that pastoral planning is really about parish triage is to not only miss the central point but to foster a view of pastoral planning that will inevitably end up weakening vitality.

Before we discuss what it means to be a vital parish, we need to understand what a parish is. Then we will paint a picture of what a vibrant parish would look and act like.

FAITH COMMUNITY AS A COMMUNION

The first thing to notice is that every parish is essentially a faith community. It will be as Ezekiel told us: dead, dry bones can be enfleshed and made to look alive; but until the Spirit enlivens them, they remain lifeless (Ez 37:1-10). A parish can have church buildings, geographic boundaries, history, members, priests, staff, and liturgies, but unless it is a community of faith, it does not live the life of the Spirit.

Not every faith community is a parish, but only a faith community can be a parish in any real sense.

A parish is a community of the baptized who have committed themselves to follow Jesus Christ as Redeemer. Through baptism, each is incorporated into the Body of Christ. We enter a new life in the Spirit. In a mysterious but no less real way we can each say, "I have been crucified with Christ; yet I live, no longer I, but Christ lives in me" (Gal 2:20). When Jesus promised that he would be with us to the end of time, he was confirming that as long as his followers were in the world, he would be there, in and through them. This is more than a community. It is a communion of disciples in and with Jesus Christ, God the Father, and the Holy Spirit. Through this communion we become participants in the life and love of the Trinity. In a community we are part of a group; in communion we enter into a mutual life at the deepest level of our being.

Before it is anything else, a parish is a specific embodiment of Christ. It is the Body of Christ in a particular place and at a particular time. The reality of the life of Christ expresses itself through the manifold and diverse human beings that make up the Body. What does such a community look and act like?

BAPTISM AND EUCHARIST AT THE CENTER

A vital faith community focuses on and finds its identity in the two great sacraments: Baptism and Eucharist. Baptism is not seen as only a rite of initiation or as a social and family event, but is a life-generating event in the life of each baptized person and of the community. Each time a person professes faith in Jesus Christ as savior and redeemer and undergoes the sacramental death and new life of Baptism, the entire community participates again in the ongoing incarnation of Jesus. In a vital parish, every Baptism takes place within and before the faith community so that the Baptism of each is seen and celebrated as incorporation into the Body of Christ and as sacrament of the ongoing incorporation of all members. The continuing life of the Body of Christ is energized and fed by the Eucharist as Bishop Matthew H. Clark of Rochester, New York reminds us.

> In this action of praise and proclamation, offering and receiving, we know Jesus present in the midst of the assembly, in the proclamation of the Word and in the bread and wine, now the Body and Blood of Christ. In this Eucharistic action we are fed and nourished so as to go out into the world to be the presence of Christ, to live Christ's dying and rising in our worlds of family and friends, work and play, neighbor and stranger.
>
> —*Centrality of Eucharist: From East to West a Perfect Offering*

This sacramental mystery is the fundamental sign of our common life in Jesus. As a sacrament it is both sign and cause of that life and the unity based on it.

Because of this focus on Baptism and Eucharist, churches are filled to overflowing for the Easter Triduum in vibrant parishes. The importance of Baptism and Eucharist will have led to a desire to celebrate both those sacraments in ways that contribute to the vitality of the Church and to join with all those in a regional area who are incorporated in the Body of Christ.

DIVERSITY

Vital faith communities more clearly reflect the diversity and richness of the larger community. They are noted for their hospitality and sense of welcoming. "All are welcome here" is their byword. The only requirement for membership is faith as expressed in the creed. Socioeconomic status, age, race, color, sexual orientation, disabling conditions, health, addictions, and gender are irrelevant to full and complete membership. Further, a vital faith community recognizes and celebrates all these differences as evidence that the spirit of Christ is actively present in the community.

Faith communities near campus ministry communities include them in Sunday Eucharist. Those near prisons and jails include the incarcerated faithful who are not able to be present physically. Priests serving vital parishes collaborate to provide regular Mass at local prisons and jails. Because these Masses are primarily on weekdays rather than Sundays, parishioners join with the prison communities in these celebrations just as they regularly volunteer in the pastoral care of these communities. Those who are ill or infirm are remembered as well. Many are present through telecommunication. Each week members of the community visit all those who are not able to be present physically. These visits often, but not always, include Holy Communion.

RESPONSE TO CHANGE

Vital faith communities have an amazing ability to sense and respond to change. Their members understand the need for both stability and adaptability. The communities are "ever new and ever the same" because they have developed ways of thinking about what must always stay the same and what must always be in transition.

It is the gospel, the "good news," that always stays the same. The good news of Jesus Christ, as expressed in scripture and through the long tradition of faithful people, never changes. As the history of the Church has taught them, however, believers must understand this good news and live it in a human and physical environment that constantly changes. While the core message never changes, reflecting the eternal nature of God and God's love for us, that message also reflects the ongoing incarnation of God as human and of the incorporation of believers into the Body of Christ. This ongoing incarnation and incorporation will reflect and interact with the world as it is at any specific time.

STUDY AND LEARNING

Vital parishes and faith communities are known as places of study and learning. From childhood through one's final days, the members have an almost unquenchable thirst to learn about God, Jesus Christ, the Church, and human spirituality. As they creatively struggle to bring the good news to their world, they seek understanding and comfort from the scriptures and from the long tradition of faithful people who have struggled as they do. They leave no stone unturned in their desire to know and appreciate the vast and diverse tradition of the Church. They look at scripture and tradition as the means by which they can construct the Church suited for their time and their place, just as their ancestors in faith did in their own circumstances. They turn to the past not to find "the right answer" but to create their own answers in ways that flow from the history of God's relation with humanity. Some members have obtained certification and/or advanced education so that they might lead others in this learning process in a wide variety of settings: religious education for children, sacramental preparation, youth ministry, and adult faith formation calibrated to the stages of life.

LITURGY, PREACHING, AND PRAYER

The worship of vital communities is active, alive, and attractive. Partially-filled churches are seen as almost insurmountable barriers to energetic and life-giving worship. Vital parishes easily revise Mass schedules so that, whenever and wherever possible, the entire faith community gathers as one for Sunday Eucharist. The community insists that each liturgy be well planned and well executed. Members of the assembly serve in a wide variety of roles, each of which is considered a ministry: hospitality, cross bearers, candle bearers, lectors, Eucharistic ministers, ushers, cantors, musicians, choristers, sacristans, bread bakers, and others. Members prepare for these ministries by training and praying together regularly. Individuals prepare for each liturgy, and the assembled participate actively in each liturgy. Visitors often comment on the spirit of the community evident in the liturgy itself.

Preaching is varied, focused, and well executed. Those preaching prepare by meeting regularly with members of the parish to discuss the Sunday readings and the themes and issues that arise from them. These sessions ensure that preaching addresses the experience of the baptized in their efforts to be in the world but not of the world. Those who preach regularly receive feedback on both content and delivery to assist them in their continuous improvement.

The community looks for reasons to come together in prayer and liturgy in addition to Sunday Eucharist. Members have a variety of liturgical and devotional opportunities to come together in public, liturgical prayer. The communities are also known as prayerful communities, not just for their commitment to public prayer but also for their devotion to personal prayer and small-group faith sharing. Prayer ties the parish together and is the foundation for community in the midst of a wonderful diversity.

BEATITUDES IN ACTION

As important as all of the above is, these parishes and faith communities find their true meaning by extending beyond the church into the world as the Body of Christ. The most important characteristic of this extension, this presence, is its exuberance. It is as though they really have no choice; the vitality of their faith naturally overflows into the world with a commitment to gospel living. They are clear examples—both as individual members and as entire communities—of Paul's insight that baptism brings us into a new life in which "I live no longer I, but Christ lives in me." (Gal 2:20). This new life of Christ becomes the life that the Church and the faithful express.

Vibrant parishes are vivid examples of the Beatitudes in action. Each parish pursues a varied agenda of social justice and action. Through a variety of organizations and mechanisms, they give evidence that Jesus—the Christ into whom they have been incorporated—is present and active in the world, working for justice and mercy for the weak and vulnerable among us. Members understand their call to express God's love for all in their own personal lives and work. As individuals, they are involved in a variety of secular organizations that work for peace and justice. The parish itself is also involved in direct action or in supporting individuals and organizations that work for peace and justice. Parishes continually review the most recent information on the human and spiritual conditions of the communities they serve. They make the best possible use of socioeconomic information and regularly update parish information through a parish visitation program. Based on this information, they creatively design ministry programs that address the current needs of the community. Moreover, they are willing to change those ministries as human and spiritual conditions change.

UNION WITH THE LARGER CHURCH

Each vibrant parish has a strong and active identity that is achieved through collaboration with other communities. Just like an emotionally healthy person, autonomy provides the basis for effective and life-giving relationships with others. Vital parishes easily and creatively collaborate with other parishes and faith communities. They celebrate their faithful union with other parishes in the diocese and through the diocese with the worldwide Church. This union is one of faith, love, and mercy, and does not focus on uniformity in thought and practice. There is a graced ability to accept others, live comfortably with ambiguity, and focus on the important things that bring people of faith together rather than on those that separate them.

JOYFULNESS

In the end, it is joyfulness that seems to best characterize these vital parish communities. There is a pervading sense of joy based on faith that God exists and loves us, that Jesus saves us, and that together we work for the Reign of God that has been established but has not yet fully flowered. It is a joy that is not based on a lack of problems, challenges, difficulties, disagreements, disappointments, and sorrows; there are plenty of these. Rather, it is a joy based on faith, a joy that thrives in spite of overwhelming evidence to the contrary. In the end, the only way to explain such a community is to see it as an incarnation of God and the Spirit of life and love.

SUMMARY

Our review of parish vitality leads us in interesting directions. Clearly, quantitative measures of the assets and activities of a parish, while important, cannot measure vitality, the life expressed through our gracious and free response to the Spirit. Regardless of how much a parish has, its vitality resides in what it is and what it does. We saw that a qualitative description works best. It always seems to come back to the same insight: The vitality of a faith community arises from its acceptance of itself as the Body of Christ and the extent to which its members are in communion with each other and with the Trinity.

What Is the Work and Character of Effective Pastoral Councils?

Others have written comprehensively about pastoral councils and their role in the Church (see Gubish and Fischer in Appendix A). The 1983 revision of the *Code of Canon Law* sought to implement the ecclesiology articulated by Vatican II. For the first time, canon law addressed the need for and the work of pastoral councils. Subsequent writings have pointed out the advisability of the use of pastoral councils to support the work of the church at all levels.

A pastoral council is a group of the faithful that is broadly representative of the faith community. It investigates and ponders significant pastoral issues and develops creative and effective responses to those issues. A pastoral council reads the signs of the times and devises the actions of the faith community, the Body of Christ, to respond to the discerned pastoral issues and needs. The essential work of a pastoral council is to participate with the pastor or pastoral leader in thinking and praying about these actions. In short, the central work of a pastoral council is pastoral planning.

In the following sections, we will discuss the type of people who will make a pastoral council effective, the relationship between the council and the pastoral leader, the authority of a council, and the crucial role of collaboration.

MEMBER CHARACTERISTICS

The membership of a pastoral council should be broadly representative of the community of faith and yet small enough to be effective. Members should be active in the faith community and in good standing. A pastoral council is a team. What we know about effective teams applies to pastoral councils: team members must have personal characteristics that contribute to team effectiveness. While there are many characteristics, two are relatively more important. First, members should be clearly focused on the mission of the faith community, or at least open to a formation that would create that commitment. It is tantalizingly easy to think that a pastoral council deals with the same issues as a board of directors: balance sheets, facilities, staff evaluations, and fund raising. Members of the council must be focused on the *purpose* of a faith community, not the *means*—no matter how significant they might be. In other words, members need to both understand and be personally committed to the mission of being Christ in and to the world, of announcing the good news that the Reign of God has come to embrace all—particularly those whom society ignores and marginalizes. Without that common focus, a pastoral council begins with a cloudy focus and has a difficult time seeing pastoral issues clearly.

The second characteristic of effective council members is a highly developed capacity to learn. This capacity is based on the ability to listen to others and to accept information in a way that opens us to changing even our strongly held opinions and positions. A council will typically be composed of people who have opinions and positions on issues. The key is that we can hold these gently enough so we can hear different and often conflicting viewpoints and thus be open to coming to different positions that integrate our past experience with new understandings. This requires a learning stance toward others, not a stance that focuses on convincing others of our own position. It requires us to listen to the small voice in the back of our head that gently whispers, "You might be wrong." Surely this could only be the work of grace!

A council composed of people who are committed to the mission of Jesus Christ and who are open to learning about themselves, others, and the world will have the human resources necessary for effective pastoral planning.

RELATIONSHIP TO THE PASTOR

In a real sense, it is the relationship to a pastor that makes a council pastoral. A pastoral council relates to a pastor (priest, pastoral administrator, bishop) in its work of identifying pastoral issues and recommending creative responses. With the renewal begun by Vatican II, many dioceses and parishes created "parish councils" shortly after the council concluded. These were to provide at least one way for the Church to exhibit her reclaimed understanding as the People of God in addition to her hierarchical authority structure. Unfortunately, many of these councils were formed before a theology of pastoral councils was worked out. Most of them began to look and act like boards of trustees of non-profit organizations and to take on decisions that were not theirs, strictly speaking. In addition, they often focused on administrative and coordinating roles rather than on the pastoral planning envisioned by the council and articulated in the 1983 revision of canon law.

This situation did not typically develop because councils sought to extend their authority, but rather because pastors sought to expand the role of the laity in the church by delegating authority that canonically belonged to them. Councils have consultative or recommending roles, with the actual decision maker being the pastoral leader. The result has often been confusion about the role of a pastoral council and its relationship to pastors.

In American culture, the role of voluntary associations (noted by D'Tocqueville in the nineteenth century) and formal not-for-profit corporations has created a theory and practice of governance of such organizations. This governance system is based on self-perpetuating boards of trustees who have fiduciary responsibility for the well-being of the organization, for resources entrusted (gifted) to the organizations, and, importantly, for the public interest. Pastoral councils are *not* such bodies in today's church.

AUTHORITY

The Roman Catholic Church views authority in often ambiguous ways. It combines both the formal authority of its hierarchical structure with the more communitarian authority of the Church as the People of God. Surely no one would take the position that the hierarchy in and of itself constitutes the Church; a Church without the People of God makes little sense. At the same time, a Church without principles of formal authority makes little sense as well. In the Roman Catholic tradition, authority is enfleshed in the hierarchical structure of Pope, bishops, and pastors. Each of these levels has authority within its sphere. How these two types of authority—hierarchical and communitarian—are integrated peacefully and effectively is a central question for the contemporary church. Clearly, the answer is not the affirmation of one to the exclusion of the other, but rather to live flexibly and astutely with both and to seek integration in the mission of Jesus Christ rather than in some final settlement of the "governance question."

Pastoral councils are part of this tension and integration. Even though the authority of councils is dependent on the authority and role of pastor and bishop, they have standing and authority in their own right as expressions of the communion of disciples of Jesus Christ.

COLLABORATION

The key to an effective pastoral council and to its integration into the life of the Church is a commitment to collaboration and collaborative ministry. Such collaboration is based on a commitment to the mission of Jesus Christ, which is the mission of the Church. In fact, the Church exists for the mission of Jesus Christ; it is the means to that end. While authority is necessary for concerted human action, it needs to be an authority that serves rather than an authority that is concerned with maintaining and strengthening itself. Church authority must always serve the mission to which Jesus calls his disciples.

As L. Sofield and C. Juliano have pointed out, collaboration is based on a full and complete reliance on the gifts of the assembly of the faith community and the promise of Jesus that whatever we need will be provided to that assembly. Instead of assuming that the talents and gifts are disproportionately distributed to those in formal positions of authority, collaboration understands that gifts are distributed as the Spirit wills without the distinctions of class or status. Thus, a faith community that assumes greater gifts among those in authority is not open to the full range of the power of the Spirit within it and thus not fully open to collaboration.

Collaboration begins with this understanding of the gifts of the spirit but adds three essential elements: discernment, development, and application. An effective pastoral council will be open to the gifts and wisdom of all. It will foster a process by which members of the assembly discern their gifts and the needs of the community. It will likewise foster formal processes for the development of the gifts of the assembly and for the full application of those gifts in service to the faith community and in the mission of Jesus Christ.

SUMMARY

Pastoral councils are to be an essential feature of the Church at all levels. The proper work of a pastoral council is pastoral planning: the process of praying and thinking together about the actions of the Body of Christ in a specific time and place. In collaboration with the pastoral leader, pastoral councils provide the means for the People of God to play their proper role in the leadership of the community of disciples.

An Overview of Pastoral Planning at Three Levels

Pastoral planning occurs at all levels and situations in the Church since we are all and everywhere called to be the hands of the Body of Christ in the world. However, we will be focusing here on processes for pastoral planning on three primary levels: diocesan, parish, and regional groupings. The following is brief discussion of each.

DIOCESAN

Although many Catholics think of their parish when they hear the term "local church," this term properly applies to the diocese and the bishop who presides over it. While a parish is typically the setting in which most Catholics experience the Church, the parish exists by virtue of the diocese of which it is a part. Just as the diocese is a constituent element of the universal church, so too the parish is a constituent part of the diocesan church. While much of what Catholics experience of the diocesan church appears to be administrative, the fundamentals of parish faith community flow from the diocese and its presiding bishop.

Thus it is important that the diocesan church engage in pastoral planning: praying and thinking together about the actions of the Body of Christ in a particular time and place. A diocesan pastoral council (DPC) working in concert with a priests' council, finance council, and other consultative bodies is the proper body to carry out diocesan pastoral planning. (These bodies are fully described in chapter 6 and in Appendix B glossary.) The membership of the DPC is broadly representative of the diocese and makes recommendations to the bishop about pastoral needs and the creative responses to these needs. Much of contemporary pastoral planning in America and Canada deals with the number of and relationships among parishes, often called configuration planning. Driven to some extent by the decline in the number of priests, dioceses with declining populations and church membership, as well as those with growing populations and church membership, need to consider carefully how to best respond to these situations.

In addition to these more pastoral issues, dioceses as large-scale organizations face significant issues of resource acquisition and allocation. These types of issues are typically addressed through strategic planning with its emphasis on resource acquisition. This type of planning is a powerful means of positioning an organization within a competitive marketplace—in this case, a marketplace of ideas and allegiance. The driver of strategic planning is the scarcity of available resources in the external environment of an organization. Change and adaptation are required to ensure that an organization continues to exist in a way that permits it to continue its work on behalf of its mission.

There is an inherent and powerful relationship between pastoral planning and Christian stewardship. Initially, we might think this relationship is based on stewardship as the source of the resources—time, talent, and money—needed by the faith community as it implements the results of pastoral planning, the acts of the Body of Christ in a particular time and place. However, the more fundamental relationship is the spiritual source of both pastoral planning and stewardship. Pastoral planning proceeds from an understanding of our relationship with God as disciples called by Jesus Christ to announce the Reign of God. As disciples, we are formed into a communion with other disciples and with the Father, Son, and Holy Spirit so that we participate sacramentally in the mutual love of the Trinity. This body of disciples constitutes the Body of Christ, who acts in the world through and within us.

Stewardship is a notion based on a profound recognition of our giftedness by God and an overwhelming sense of gratitude. This is an existential giftedness and gratitude. God gifts us with life itself, regardless of the circumstances or conditions of our life. Whether we are rich or poor, healthy or sick, powerful or weak, known or unknown, God has blessed and gifted us with life itself, life that is an expression of God's own life and love.

In addition, some of us have been blessed with gifts of health, talents, understanding, riches, and position. Flowing from this existential gratitude, we understand that these gifts and many more are not ours in the sense that they are for our exclusive use. Rather, we are blessed with these gifts in order to place them at the service of God through the communion of disciples, the Body of Christ. In a sense, pastoral planning answers this question: to what purpose is my gratitude to be expressed? Pastoral planning without stewardship fails to achieve its full potential. Stewardship without pastoral planning faces the same fate. Chapter 5 will discuss diocesan pastoral planning in more detail.

PARISH/FAITH COMMUNITY

A parish or other stable faith community (campus ministry and other specialized ministry communities) is the fundamental manifestation of the Body of Christ active in the world. Here disciples gather to build up their community of faith so that individually and in groups they are empowered and emboldened to go about the work of announcing the Reign of God. Parishes, as the enfleshment of the Body of Christ on the very local level, also face the impact of social and religious change directly and sharply. They must be constantly sensing changes and adapting to them so that the work of the Reign of God continues in reality.

Parish pastoral councils are either the body that does pastoral planning or sponsors that planning with a specially designed and empowered pastoral planning team. Either way it is the pastoral council that affirms the next best steps for the Body of Christ in a particular time and place. Just as the connection with stewardship is essential at the diocesan level, it is also significant at the parish level as well. Chapter 6 will discuss parish pastoral planning in more detail.

INTERMEDIARY OR REGIONAL GROUPINGS

While the American Church has had vicariates or deaneries for some time, these administrative subdivisions of dioceses serve a relatively obscure and often ceremonial function in the Church. These regional groupings eased some of the administrative burdens of the Church. As dioceses began to face the realities of declining numbers of priests and the shifting of populations from central cores to suburban and more rural areas, many began to reinvigorate the older structures. Some dioceses created new regional structures specifically designed to support pastoral planning by smaller groups of parishes: typically two to as many as six. Almost always these parishes were geographically contiguous and served relatively similar types of populations. (See *The Church in the City Project of the Diocese of Cleveland* for an example of non-geographic approach, www.citc.org.)

While these groups faced similar issues and problems and were often given projections of priests and other resources over five to ten years, they faced the task of pastoral planning without any functioning infrastructure of collaboration. As a result, those that succeeded developed pastoral councils representative of the constituent parishes and faith community and worked out operating procedures based on principles of pastoral councils but tailored to these new situations.

The authority of these councils in themselves and in relationship to the member parishes, members, and pastors required new understandings and procedures never envisioned by canon law. The most effective groups have been those that took the radical position that all plans and actions had to be affirmed by the pastoral councils of all members in concert with the pastors. While this runs the risk of providing each community a veto over any concerted action, it is the only realistic way of developing plans that will be implemented. Any plan that is only imposed by authority will ultimately not be fully implemented.

Perhaps the role of diocesan staff is nowhere more important than in working with these groups so that they come to successful conclusions and understandings. Chapter 7 will discuss regional pastoral planning in more detail.

Conclusion

This chapter has provided an introduction to pastoral planning. We looked at the elements of a simple definition of pastoral planning: the process of praying and thinking together about the actions of the Body of Christ in a specific time and place. This gave us a basic view of pastoral planning and the ways in which it is similar to and different from secular planning. We reviewed the question of the vitality of a parish and learned that vitality is really an expression of the action of the Spirit within disciples rather than measures of things and activities. We reviewed the nature of pastoral councils (membership, relationship to pastoral leaders, authority, and collaboration) and their essential role in pastoral planning. Finally we took a quick look at the three levels of pastoral planning that will be the focus of this book: diocese, parish, and region. We turn in the next chapter to some fundamental notions about planning.

Study Questions

1. With what aspects of the definition of pastoral planning do you agree? With which do you disagree? Why?
2. How would you describe a vibrant faith community? How does your current parish/faith community measure up to that description?
3. In what ways could the members of your pastoral council or planning team share their faith more easily and gracefully?
4. In what ways does it make sense to say that the proper work of a pastoral council is pastoral planning?
5. In what ways are your pastoral council meetings lively and joyful? In what ways are they routine and predictable? Which seems more likely to be an expression of the Spirit of God within and among you?
6. What questions does the discussion of authority in the Church raise for you?

CHAPTER 2

Pastoral Planning Basics

It is tempting to proceed immediately from a *decision* to do pastoral planning to actually *doing* pastoral planning. "We need to figure out our pastoral priorities and plans. Let's get it done next month." This enthusiastic but naive approach may satisfy our need to act on a perceived problem, but it will inevitably result in a flawed process that often does more harm than good. Every unsuccessful planning effort fails to deal with the issues or problems that stimulated the planning in the first place. More important, however, it makes it more difficult to plan effectively in the future because people recall the failed effort and especially those who were responsible for it.

In this chapter we will first discuss some important planning considerations that will help us be more realistic and pragmatic in our planning. Secondly, we will develop a way to think about the key areas of pastoral concern, the focus for pastoral planning. Finally, we will review the characteristics of effective pastoral planning that leads to both real change and improvement in the quality of the pastoral life of a faith community. No pastoral planning, no matter how well designed and implemented, is effective unless it results in a better faith community, one that comes closer to the ideals of the disciples of Jesus Christ.

With these concepts in our minds and spirits, we will move in subsequent chapters to a description of the process of pastoral planning at the three levels of the local Church: parish, region, and diocese.

Important Planning Considerations

While pastoral planning is different in important ways from other kinds of planning, we can learn important lessons from the way secular organizations practice planning. The following are six insights that will help avoid some common planning pitfalls.

EFFECTIVE PLANNING REQUIRES A PROCESS.

Planning even the simplest task or set of tasks can be complex and confusing, especially if there are other people

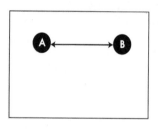

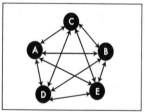

involved. The complexity of any project increases geometrically with the number of people involved. A two-person team deals with two relationships: A with B, and B with A. A team of five people deals with at least ninety-five different relationships: A with each of B, C, D, E as well as A with B and C, B and D, etc. A interacting with B while C is observing will be different from A interacting with B while D or E is observing. With more people and more communication exchanges come more opportunities for miscommunication and misunderstanding. Both of these tend to reverberate and amplify through even a relatively small human system.

If the task itself is at all complex, the very thought of engaging in a process that will produce an effective outcome is sometimes overwhelming. A clearly communicated process along with a common vocabulary can make an otherwise impossible task at least thinkable. When individuals and especially teams approach a task for the first time, it is essential that they have a path forward. Eventually they will modify, reject, or completely accept the process, but without a starting point, a group facing a new task runs the risk of never being able to get started.

While effective planning requires a process, it is important that the process be the simplest process consistent with achieving results. No one would think of using the highly complex process used to plan space travel to plan a family vacation. And no one would use the family vacation process to plan a shuttle launch. There is a judgment point at which we have just enough but not too much process. Too little or too much process and the project never materializes. As a general rule, it is wiser to begin with a little too much process and then streamline rather than start with a process that is too lean. Any project manager will tell you that it is easier to loosen up than to tighten up once a project is underway.

Leadership is responsible for creating an initial path forward, especially for a group that is approaching planning for the first time. This process (examples will be described later) needs to be clear, easy to understand, and easy to communicate to others. Flow charts can be helpful in presenting the process and in tracking progress. The challenge for leadership is that this initial process must be both clear and workable enough to be an effective starting point, and yet flexible enough to allow those involved to adjust the process as they make the process their own. Often this is more of an issue for the style of leadership.

PLANNING IS ABOUT CHANGE.

We need to plan because our world and we ourselves constantly change. Heraclitus (Greek philosopher, sixth century BCE) observed that you can never put your foot into the same stream twice. Since the water is constantly flowing, every foot placement finds a "new" stream, one that had never existed before and will never exist again. While this has always been true, it seemed somehow less unsettling when we and our world did not change all that much from one generation to another. While it was true that everything was in flux, the solutions to problems that worked yesterday, last year, last century still worked well enough today that we didn't have to come up with new ways of dealing with reality. In contemporary society, the scope and pace of change require constant planning. The problems do not stay the same, let alone the solutions.

Of course, this does not mean that everything is relative. Our core beliefs and values—our call from Jesus Christ and the working of the Spirit in us—remain constant and unchanging. However, just as there is a fundamental difference between first-century Palestine and twenty-first-century Los Angeles, our planning has to take this reality into account. Humans change; cultures change; the physical environment changes. Our call is the same, but it will look and feel different depending on the time and place: the signs of the times.

Within this context, it is contradictory to think of planning as a way to keep things the same or as a way to return to the way things used to be. Both of those very human desires are essentially based on an illusion that our world is composed of things that somehow do not or should not change. Of course, we would like to think that because it would mean that we do not or would not have to change. Effective planning cannot be based on illusions but must be based on a clear-headed engagement with the way things are.

Because the world and we ourselves are constantly changing, we have compelling evidence that what we did yesterday to resolve issues and challenges no longer works as well today. We have to invent new approaches to new challenges. Planning is about this invention and implementation.

EFFECTIVE PLANNING IS BASED ON AGREEMENT ABOUT THE PRESENT.

Most people think that planning deals with the future. "We are here. We want to be there. Planning will help us identify the path to get there." We spend most of our time trying to agree on where we want to be and assume that everyone knows where we are. After all, we are all here, in the same place. Right? Wrong.

In fact, it turns out that the key to effective planning is for us to agree on where we are right now. The scope and pace of change makes this a challenge. We all have filters and models that we use to organize reality lest the undifferentiated nature of physical and social reality overwhelm us. We need to know what to pay attention to out of the mass of stimuli that bombard us constantly. We construct our own reality based on our past experiences of what works and what does not. Unfortunately, most of the time we are living in the past, thinking it is the present, and trying to plan for the future. This is where information about present realities is so important. It forces us to take a careful look at the way things are, not how they were or how we would like them to be. This is not easy and often fails because it requires us to give up our preconceived notions of how things are and how they came to be. If we can give these up, however, we can learn. Learning is the only sure path to effective planning.

"NO ONE OF US IS AS SMART AS ALL OF US."

This saying is a fundamental truth of effective planning (See Blanchard and Parisi-Carew in Appendix A). In any team or planning group, there are some people with more power and authority. Sometimes this power is based on position, and sometimes it is based on personal characteristics and skills. Intelligence, insight, commitment, honesty, creativity, and other important talents and gifts are not necessarily more present in people with formal power and authority. Yet, left to our own devices, these people will unduly influence us, often to the detriment of the overall result. It is important that an effective planning process be attentive to involving all members. There are a number of relevant group process techniques that help "level the playing field" by not giving an advantage to those who are more aggressive and assertive, but not necessarily more intelligent and creative.

Those of us with positions of formal authority must be careful not to use that position, even unintentionally, to determine the outcome of the process. People will tend to naturally defer to someone who is an authority or someone who is in a position of authority—not necessarily the same thing. Since it is essential that all participants feel they are legitimate actors in the process, leaders must be careful to express their views or provide information in a way that does not stifle the engagement of others.

QUALITY IS MORE IMPORTANT THAN QUANTITY.

Although those in ministry tend to think that business organizations are only interested in quantity, most of these organizations have learned that only quality counts. Focusing on quantitative measurements, especially on short-term numerical goals, can prove deadly to an organization. While the current impact of stockholders and their demand for short-term earnings has challenged this insight, it remains true that quality drives everything. It is important to understand quality as meeting or exceeding the needs and expectations of those we serve. In the end, this is what drives successful organizations, not the numerical targets that make us think we are being realistic and pragmatic.

In fact, the use of short-term numerical targets without clear methodological changes is a recipe for disaster. Saying that we are going to increase some rate by 25 percent is meaningless unless we can explain why a 25 percent increase is important and can specify what we will do differently that a reasonable person would think could result in such a change. No matter what goal we set for ourselves, if we continue to do things the same old way, we will continue to get the same old results.

TWO KINDS OF PLANNING: DIRECTIVE AND PROBABLISTIC.

There are basically two approaches to planning: directive and probabilistic. We are most familiar with the directive model: we are here, we want to be there, and this is what we need to do to get there. This approach assumes that we

know where we are and where we want to be and that we can control our movement toward the desired state. It assumes that the major variables controlling our reality are under our control. All we need to do is focus on what we want and then implement action steps that will move us in that direction. While it is often true that looking back from the present tends to confirm this view, our ability to control our reality is so limited that planning can seem useless. Nevertheless, this approach to planning is the dominant one. We continue to use this model because it comforts us to think that what we decide and what we do determine our circumstances even though we have evidence to the contrary.

The other type of planning is probabilistic. This approach assumes that no single person or set of persons controls what happens to themselves or others. In fact, the best we can do is to make probabilistic projections of likely futures using the best information available. Some of this information describes the efforts we will be making to achieve some desired state, but this approach assumes that there are multiple other factors that will influence the final outcome. In fact, a chart of probabilistic planning would look more like a weather forecast map than the linear process shown previously. In this approach, it is important to know where you are and where you would like to go, but it forswears linear action steps to that goal. It is a more organic approach that assumes each step closer to the desired state results in a changed perspective that then provides a new way of looking at the future and thus of selecting the next step.

In times of little change over the planning horizon, the first approach is workable. However, in times of rapid and radical change, the directive approach is doomed to ineffectiveness. We need an approach that tolerates ambiguity, is flexible both with regard to means and ends, and values diversity.

Implications for Pastoral Planning

These six insights about planning come from planning experience in a wide variety of organizations and institutions. What are the implications for pastoral planning?

Vatican II urged us to read the signs of the times and to create and sustain faithful communities of disciples who would follow Jesus in whatever conditions their world would present. We are bound together and forever in the faith, the personal relationship with Jesus, who always acts in us as human beings, as members of human communities. In the early church, these communities were small, highly personal, and often in a state of crisis. The Church today is a human institution that requires the astute use of the best human wisdom about how to create and sustain concerted action toward organizational goals.

There should be no misunderstanding about this. We are Church because God has called us to announce the Reign of God to the world and especially to those about whom the world cares little. Moreover, our work to announce God's reign will involve each of us in our own personal paschal mystery, our own cycle of death and new life, of failure and faithful persistence. But we are also called to use our best human talents and understanding on behalf of this community seeking its life in the death and resurrection of Jesus the Christ.

The conjunction of our human understanding of organizations with our graced response to God's call means that we come to a joyful understanding that we are disciples in and through a very human institution. Concerted action even in a single parish requires a clear process so that the talents and gifts of all the assembly can be placed into the service of the mission. Pastoral planning joyfully confronts change in the conditions under which we are called to discipleship. The ministry of our parents and grandparents may well not be the ministry needed by today's conditions. As Christians, we are members of the Body of Christ called to do the work of God in the world: each and every one of us is called and has a role to play. Pastoral planning must be done in such a way that the talents and gifts of the assembly are discovered, called forth, respected, and celebrated. Not only does top down, command-and-control planning not work anymore, it is fundamentally at odds with an understanding of the Church as the people of God.

Although we count many things in pastoral planning, we cannot measure quantitatively the most important thing: the vibrancy of a faith community. The heart of pastoral planning is a focus on qualitative issues without ignoring the quantitative. Finally, the notion of probabilistic planning helps us understand that pastoral planning must be an essential and ongoing part of the life of a vibrant faith community. Pastoral planning is not "done" with a five-year plan but is an ongoing cyclical process.

Key Areas of Pastoral Concern

Just as we need models and categories to help us deal with the bewildering diversity of reality, we also need some schema to help us approach pastoral issues in a way that makes sense. There are several different schemas for this purpose. No one is perfect. Many dioceses—either through pastoral councils, synods, or local legislation—have spelled out the areas of pastoral concern to which parishes and faith communities are called. A parish should ensure that it is in harmony with any such diocesan approach. This will facilitate healthy collaboration with other parishes using the same approach.

The *Code of Canon Law* provides us with some important definitions. "A parish is a definite community of Christian faithful established on a stable basis within" a diocese. "The pastoral care of the parish is entrusted to a pastor . . . under the authority of the diocesan bishop" (c. 5151). The *Code* speaks of pastoral care as composed of teaching, sanctifying, and governing (c. 528–529). The pastor and those who join him either as lay ecclesial ministers or as members of the assembly provide for the ongoing care and life of the parish so that it engages in the work of Jesus and supports individual members in their call to live the gospel in their lives in the world.

While there are many models that provide schemas for reviewing the pastoral life of a parish, the following five-element schema has proven its usefulness in both parish and diocesan pastoral planning: word, worship, community, service, and temporalities. By extension these five areas can be used to view faith communities at all three levels: parish, region, and diocese.

WORD

Each faith community formed as disciples of Jesus Christ is based in scripture, tradition, and the teaching of the Church. A vibrant faith community is focused on the Word in these multiple manifestations. The members of such a community not only hear the Word preached in a quality manner but also are also individually devoted to reading and praying the Word. Importantly, they are also committed to passing on this understanding and prayerful formation to the younger members of the community. Faith formation appropriate to all ages and levels of development, including adults, is an ongoing part of the ministry of the Word.

WORSHIP

Catholic Christian communities are formed in their very essence by the Eucharist and are nourished by sacraments and the rich devotional tradition of the Church. These public expressions of faith are both signs and causes of a deepening of God's life in the members of the community. Both communal and individual prayer life is essential to the vitality and vibrancy of a Catholic Christian community. Vatican II taught us that the ideal is the "full, active, and conscious" participation of all in the liturgy. By extension this ideal applies to all worship and prayer of a vibrant faith community. Unless parishes are to become homogeneous gatherings of people with certain ways to pray and worship, a vibrant parish should embrace a diversity of prayer and worship styles.

COMMUNITY

As Christians we always journey in the company of other believers, other disciples. As human beings we exist in community with others. These human communities do not happen automatically, nor do they necessarily achieve their highest ideals. Each community is a human culture that requires sustenance and care. A vibrant faith community is one that has a deep and complex human life that values each individual member and attends to the health and functioning of the community itself.

SERVICE

We are not called as disciples of Jesus Christ to read and pray the Word, to worship well, and to enrich our human community as though these were ends in themselves. Ultimately, we follow Jesus who made it quite clear that he and each of us are called to do works of justice and mercy in the world in which we find ourselves. This work is to focus especially on those who are rejected by the world. A vibrant faith community lives the fullness of its life outside its church and even outside its own confines. Study of the word, vibrant worship, and a strong community are to enable precisely these works in the world. A vital community supports ministries that pursue this work, but it also values and supports its individual members, straining to do acts of justice and mercy in the everyday reality of their lives and work in the world.

TEMPORALITIES

We are an incarnational church. We believe that God became a human being, fully and completely. God faced all the issues of human life just as we do and just as faith communities do. We need food, shelter, pastoral care, art, beauty, programs of service, liturgy, and education. All these require communities to have financial, human, and physical resources in order to fulfill their destiny as disciples of Jesus Christ. While these things can never be the bottom line for a faith community, it is necessary that these resources be sufficient for the accomplishment of the mission of the community. The proper management and stewardship of whatever resources a faith community has is also essential. We must be good stewards.

Characteristics of Effective Pastoral Planning

Whether at the diocesan, regional, or parish level, effective pastoral planning has five characteristics. Each characteristic is important, but taken together, they provide a synergy and dynamism that will produce focused, realistic, and achievable plans that will result in faith communities living their mission in greater depth.

COMPREHENSIVE

By its very nature pastoral planning deals with the totality of the discipleship to which communities are called. It begins with an understanding of mission, fundamental values, and the call of Jesus Christ. While it may be tempting to focus initially on a specific issue or problem, effective programs begin by taking a comprehensive look at the life of the faith community and the realities within which it exists. No programs, processes, ministries, or people are left out of initial consideration. All activities are subject to a thorough reexamination in light of the gospel call to do justice and mercy in the actual circumstances the community faces. A comprehensive approach, particularly at the diocesan level, helps all communities understand that they are all in this together. All face the need to continually reassess their ministries in light of changed circumstances.

SUFFICIENT RESOURCES

Comprehensive pastoral planning requires a commitment of additional time and attention. The classic planning mistake is to undertake a planning process believing that it can be accomplished in addition to all current activities. The hard reality is that either additional resources must be committed or some normal activities must be discontinued or deemphasized in order to carry out effective planning. Failure to do this results in incomplete or ill-conceived plans that end up never being implemented. When planning is added to already overburdened staff or volunteers, it becomes an unwelcome and unforeseen responsibility rather than an opportunity to prayerfully and creatively think about the demands of radical discipleship.

INVOLVEMENT OF THOSE AFFECTED

Any effective plan is a vehicle for people to change their behavior, either to solve a problem or to achieve an ideal more fully. Thus, the ultimate success of any planning process depends on the commitment and engagement of those who will implement it. The days of deductive planning—"I am in charge. I know best. Do this."—are long gone, at least in contemporary America and Canada. Vatican II taught that the Church is the People of God called by Jesus Christ to be priests, prophets, and kings. The People of God must be involved from the beginning of planning, including identification of mission, specification of objectives, and implementation of action plans. Sometimes this involvement is direct and personal; other times it is more indirect. The minimum is that the community is consistently informed of the process and has the opportunity to affirm the substance at certain critical stages.

EFFECTIVE LEADERSHIP

Every effective organization requires leadership that influences the behavior of members toward organizational goals in a way that fully respects the dignity, freedom, and autonomy of each individual. A command-and-control style may have value in a crisis situation when the demands for action foreclose the option of time needed for true leadership. But even this style will prove dysfunctional once the crisis is past and people assert their need and desire for leadership that respects them.

PRAYER AND FAITH SHARING

Prayer and faith sharing form the basis for any effective pastoral planning process. Pastoral planning is the process of thinking and praying together about the actions of the Body of Christ in a specific time and place. Praying together and sharing faith experience opens participants to the action of Christ within them and in the other members of the group. While formal recited prayers have a role in communal prayer, scripture-based faith sharing is the method that opens members of the group to each other and helps them understand that pastoral planning is a different activity than the planning they may have experienced in other settings.

Conclusion

Before beginning a pastoral planning process, we need to make sure that we have positioned ourselves to be effective. First, we need to call to mind some fundamental insights about planning of any kind.

- Effective planning requires a process.
- Planning is always about change.
- Effective planning is based on agreement about the present.
- "No one of us is as smart as all of us."
- Quality is more important than quantity.
- There are two kinds of planning: directive and probabilistic.

Second, we need to be clear about a schema to help us assess the pastoral life of a faith community. While there are many schemas and no specific one is complete, we can begin by focusing on what are sometimes called the five pillars of pastoral life:

- Word
- Worship
- Community
- Service
- Temporalities

Finally, experience has shown that effective pastoral planning exhibits the following characteristics:

- It will be comprehensive and inclusive.
- Sufficient resources will be devoted, either by providing additional resources or by reallocating resources.
- The process will involve members of the community in a variety of ways.

- Those in leadership positions will exhibit a style of leadership that values and empowers all participants.
- Prayer and faith sharing form the spiritual basis of effective pastoral planning.

Study Questions

1. Of the six insights about planning, which one strikes you as the most useful? Have you had experiences with planning that would confirm or deny the validity of these insights? Call some of these experiences to mind and describe them.

2. If planning is always about change, what kind of attitude toward change itself do you have? Do you think it is constant in all areas of your life? Are there some things that never change? What are these, and why do you think they would never change?

3. As a leader, how comfortable are you in allowing people to change a process in order to make it their own? What might be some of the stumbling blocks for a leader to facilitate this?

4. It is an excellent exercise for each of us to develop our own schema to describe the pastoral life of a faith community. What does your schema look like? How does it improve on the five pillars offered here?

5. Of the five characteristics of effective pastoral planning, which one do you think would be the most challenging for you and why? For your faith community and why?

6. Write a single paragraph that describes your most important learning from this chapter. Write a single paragraph that describes the questions or issues that arise for you from reading this chapter.

CHAPTER 3

Basic Elements of a Pastoral Plan

In this chapter we will describe the five basic elements of a pastoral plan:

- Mission
- Vision
- Goals
- Objectives
- Action steps

This will prepare us for chapter 4, which will develop an ongoing generic pastoral planning cycle that will provide a path forward for any pastoral planning process. Chapters 5, 6, and 7 will apply this generic process in detail to dioceses, parishes, and regional groupings of parishes and faith communities, respectively.

Every planning process begins with a view of how things are, envisions a more desirable future, and constructs a path to move toward that future. Thus, any planning process, especially one focused on pastoral issues, must be based on a realistic appraisal of how things are, a set of beliefs and values (often very abstract) that somehow draw us into the future, and concrete actions that move us in the direction of a desired future. A planning process that lacks any of these elements will often create more problems than it solves. Without a realistic appraisal of how things are, planning will be like an untethered kite: capable of flight if grounded, but blown into all sorts of meaningless directions if not. Without a set of beliefs and values that call us to something greater, planning can devolve into increasing the efficiency (doing things right) of what we have always done without confronting the challenge of effectiveness (doing the right things). Finally, without concrete action steps that change the way we behave and the way we allocate available resources, planning can deceive us into believing that we are really changing. To avoid these traps, a pastoral planning process must have five basic elements: mission, vision, goals, objectives, and action steps.

Mission Statement

Every organization exists to do something in order to achieve some ultimate end or goal. A mission statement describes that something and that goal. For Christian organizations there is a certain difficulty with the use of the term "mission." Jesus Christ has a mission and calls us as disciples to join him in that mission. He stated his mission most succinctly by reading from Isaiah in Luke 4:18–19: "The Spirit of the Lord is upon me, because he has anointed me to bring glad tidings to the poor. He has sent me to proclaim liberty to the captives and recovery of sight to the blind, to let the oppressed go free, and to proclaim a year acceptable to the Lord." This is the mission to which each of us is called and thus to which the Church as the communion of disciples is called. This mission never changes and it leads to the fullness of the Reign of God. As we have seen, however, we exist in specific times and places. Thus, this mission unfolds in a concrete reality that differs in place and time.

When we speak of a mission statement for the Church (parish, diocesan, or regional groupings), we must articulate a mission that is idiosyncratic to our specific situation while being consistent with this existential mission of Jesus Christ. Otherwise, at every level we could simply quote Isaiah and feel we have stated our mission. What is required is a process Chris Argyris and David Schön have called "double loop learning." (See additional information in Appendix A: Resources.) We need to go back to the basics of the scripture, especially the words of Jesus; to our two-thousand years of tradition and history; and to our current realities. We can then understand anew—as though for the first time—the call of Jesus Christ. This re-understanding does not mean that the mission of Jesus has changed, but it does mean that an understanding of the mission that may have been fruitful and life-giving twenty years ago or two-hundred years ago may no longer be as fruitful. Just as those in earlier times constructed a mission out of the message and call of Jesus and the circumstances within which they found themselves, so must we.

Sometimes people will object that we should not waste time reinventing the wheel. If we can find a mission statement for a Christian faith community that seems to have worked for it, why waste time tinkering with words? We should just use that mission statement and get on to the "real work" of planning. However, some wheels need to be reinvented, not because we end up with an objectively better wheel, but because we end up with *our* wheel. The process of developing the wheel changes us and our relationships. When we are trying to understand our call to communion in discipleship, we especially need to experience a prayerful process that changes and opens us.

The following is a helpful format to craft a mission statement: to do something in such a way that something happens or is different. Such a statement makes clear what the core work of the organization is. It also provides a way to distinguish among different organizations with the same work by specifying the manner and feel of each. Finally, it focuses on what happens because of the work of the organization. It answers the "so what" question. What difference does this organization make? Perhaps some examples will be helpful:

1. The mission of St. X Parish is to worship God through creative liturgies and to deepen the spiritual life of all members in ways that reflect the teaching of the Second Vatican Council. We do this so that the parish and its members shine as beacons of justice and mercy in the world and especially in the urban core of our home city.

2. The mission of St. Y Parish is to provide a welcoming and affirming environment for those who desire a more traditional approach to liturgy and prayer in a way that affirms the diversity of the Catholic tradition. By so doing, the parish and its members announce in their ministry and lives the Good News of Jesus Christ to our village and town.

3. The mission of St. Z Parish is to provide a presence of hope and grace in our urban neighborhood in a way that is consistent with and values Latino culture. We do so to help the Church appreciate the contribution of that culture and so that the Gospel is proclaimed in word and deed to the Latino community.

Each of these mission statements is consistent with the mission of Jesus Christ. Each has as its end the proclamation of the Good News, but each uses different words and stresses different aspects of the broad reality of the Church composed of the disciples of Jesus Christ. No one statement is better than the others. The standard for any mission statement is whether or not it captures the spirit of the community. This is why a pre-existing, pro forma mission statement can never be productive. We must always make it our own. In the next chapter we will discuss some techniques for doing that.

How long should a mission statement be? There is no precise answer to that question. It should be as long as it needs to be in order to capture the spirit of the community and to be memorable. Some urge the coffee cup test: the mission statement should be one sentence that would fit on a coffee mug or t-shirt. While that has its merits, some effective mission statements have several sentences and need to because of the complexity of the organization and its ministries. However, shorter is generally better. This typically means that everything cannot be mentioned in a mission statement. If it becomes a catalog of ministries, it begins to lose its effectiveness. The most difficult part of any planning is to face the question of what not to include. There is no end to the good activities in support of our mission, but no one parish or ministry can do everything. As Archbishop Romero has told us in his prayer, there is a certain freedom in the realization that we cannot do everything, because it frees us to do some things very well. Unfortunately, our inability to let go of good, but peripheral, activities can undercut our ability to do some things at the level of quality and activity required by our mission.

Vision Statement

If a mission tells us what an organization does, a vision statement describes where the organization sees itself in the future. In order to have a clear idea about the future, it is necessary to have a clear idea about the present. When asked to think about the future, we typically extend how we think things are now into the future. It is very difficult for most of us to predict the future because most of us can imagine only versions of what we already know. Thus, true paradigm shifts—radically different ways of seeing reality—typically come as surprises. Looking back, we can easily see the signs and the path by which the past unfolded into the present, but we have difficulty reading those signs at the time.

Where do visions come from? This is an important question because it deals with the reasons why we change our behavior. A vision is by definition a picture of a future that is different from the present, a future state that requires change in order to come into being. Social science has confirmed that human behavior is need-based: we act in order to fulfill perceived needs. Sometimes others impose these needs and at other times they arise from within us. The time and energy invested to meet those needs vary with the importance of the needs to each of us.

There are two kinds of needs that can motivate behavior: unresolved problems and unrealized ideals. We are most familiar with problem-based needs and the ways in which problems can motivate us to change our behavior. Something in our lives that is important to us is not working, or not working as well as we would like. This could be a relationship, a program, a process, a project, etc. We have an amazing ability to tolerate certain levels of dysfunction without actually investing time and energy to change ourselves or the systems within which we operate. In fact, we often do not even recognize that things are not working at first because we want them to work out. Then, even once we recognize that things are not working, we seem to be able to tolerate that dysfunction quite well. Eventually, perhaps, the dysfunction becomes so great that we confront the fact that we are not getting what we need out of the situation. At that point, we either decide to withdraw from the situation or to invest resources in changing ourselves in order to change it. The importance of the need and severity of the dysfunction will determine the level of investment and the commitment to change. We will stay with the change process until the situation changes and we are getting an acceptable level of whatever we need out of it. This type of motivation begins with problem identification and understanding how to make necessary changes.

There is also the less common, but no less important, source of change: unrealized ideals. In a sense, this is also a need-based dynamic because we have a need to live up to certain ideals we hold. However, the dynamic is different and potentially more powerful. The ideal-based change tends to proceed from positive rather than problematic situations. To some extent, we are achieving our ideals but desire to increase or improve that achievement. A person who has responded to the call to Christian discipleship knows that he or she can always do more, can always be a better disciple. This improvement is a life-long process. The call to be a disciple of Jesus is a call not to a state but to a process of becoming more and more like Jesus. Such a life is one of constant change precisely because of the nature of discipleship. This ideal motivation begins with understanding and appreciating the ways in which the ideal is already being realized and is active in our life. With this perception of what we have already achieved by the grace of God, it is possible to see the ways in which one can build on them to change and grow.

A vision statement is a word picture of a future state in which either the problems are resolved or in which the ideals are more fully realized—or both. The problem-based approach does not preclude the ideal-based approach. The vision statement describes a future state in which the mission of the organization is fully or more fully realized. It is typically written in the present tense as though it has already been achieved. This helps us experience the look and feel of what our world would be like if the mission were more fully realized. It is a narrative statement and tends to be more descriptive than clinically analytical. Perhaps a few examples will help clarify:

1. St. X Parish is now worshipping as a single community at one Sunday Mass. The church is filled to capacity, and the community is considering adding a second Mass out of necessity. This is being carefully considered because of the potential impact on the unity and identity of the community that now worships as one. The assembly participates actively in the liturgy in many different ministries. The pastoral council is constantly identifying new ways for members of the community of all ages to be engaged in worship. The community is constantly experimenting with worship forms that are consistent with the traditions of the Church and that respond to the needs and desires of its very contemporary membership. The parish is comfortable with the notion of stewardship as a way of life for disciples. There is a formal process of discerning the gifts of all members of the community and the ways in which they can be placed in service to the community and its mission. Although the member-ship of the community comes from three counties, all are engaged in the social justice activities and ministries either through prayer, financial support, or active partici-pation in the ministries. The parish is known as a place where prayer of all types is encouraged and respected. This is especially true of faith-sharing in the many small groups that have formed over the past several years. St. X Parish is known as the parish that takes seriously the call to discipleship, the spiritual life of members, and actions

of justice and mercy in the community. The pastoral leaders assigned by the bishop work collaboratively with a staff composed of lay ecclesial ministers, lay leadership (especially the parish pastoral council), and parish members who feel a sense of discipleship in their own vocations in the world.

2. St. Y Parish is a parish for all those who find energy in traditional liturgies, especially the Mass. The music is based on the traditional melodies, including Gregorian chant. A classical choir and a magnificent organ support the liturgies. The Mass itself tends to be more formal and to have periods for silent reflection. There is little experimentation since this detracts from the commitment to the well-recognized liturgical expressions. The church has been remodeled to reclaim the look and feel of 125 years ago, when it was constructed. Many people are involved in the celebration in the traditional roles of lectors, extraordinary ministers of communion, ushers, and greeters. The community orients very strongly to the pastor and looks to him for guidance and spiritual insight. Prayer life follows the formal prayer of tradition, and there are many celebrations other than the Eucharist. The community is open and welcoming and encourages newcomers to experience the liturgy and to join them in their prayers. The members support the parish with resources and direct involvement in the work of announcing the Good News to those who live in their rural and small-town environment. There is a comfortable fit between the timelessness of the parish and the desire of the larger community to retain the style and pace of their lives.

3. St. Z Parish is flourishing in its ministry to the Latino community. Most of the members of the parish are first- or second-generation Americans, and many have ongoing

connections to families in their countries of origin. The pastor and pastoral staff are bilingual, and most of the liturgies and prayers are in Spanish, a language that comforts and connects with those whose first language it is. As the third generation develops, the parish has begun to provide religious instruction in both Spanish and English. The parish has a clear focus on the pastoral needs of the permanent and newly arrived Latino members, but it is also open to Anglos who find a vibrant faith community to which they can contribute and in which they can deepen their own spiritual lives. The parish is a center for the celebration of various Latino cultures in the city and is working on a plan for a Latino heritage center. While most of its ministries deal with the pastoral needs of the Latino community, the parish is a vital member of the larger church and contributes to the overall mission of the diocese.

These vision statements are not meant to describe the current reality of these parishes but rather the future to which they aspire as they focus on fulfilling their mission statements. At the same time, it is essential that a vision proceeds from a clear-eyed view of the present reality as it stretches and pulls us along into the future. There is no one single vision of a Catholic faith community and no one right way to write a vision statement. The only requirement is that a vision statement paints a picture of a future that draws people toward it. In reading the vision statement of a parish, we can experience how that community desires to implement its mission and the values that it holds most dear.

Goals

Mission and vision statements help members focus on the unique characteristics of their communities. Goals assist members in making choices among all the worthwhile projects that could be undertaken in pursuit of that mission and vision. A goal is a statement of a future state to be achieved through a set of action steps. Goals typically extend over a three- to five-year period and describe what will be different in the ongoing behavior of an organization. Goals articulate the changes that are necessary to continue to achieve the ideal expressed in the mission statement. In pastoral planning, each goal must be related to one of the five essential pastoral areas described in chapter 2 (or however we might define pastoral in the local setting) and must be consistent with the diocesan and parish mission.

Goals are succinct statements that include . . .

1. an active verb,
2. a description of what we will do, and
3. some indication of quantity or quality.

Goals are the next best steps toward the future described in the vision statement. It is not enough to say simply that we want to move toward that future. We have to select a few key initiatives that will have a reverberating impact on the entire system. One common mistake is to think that the goals must include everything that the faith community will do over the planning period. Pastoral planning is not a comprehensive planning process that seeks to align every activity of the faith community with the mission and vision. While every activity should obviously be so related, it is not the function of pastoral planning to manage that. Pastoral planning is not the same as the annual operations plan of an organization. While good management requires such a plan, it is not the domain of pastoral planning. The latter seeks systemic change, while the former concerns itself with efficient management.

The number of goals included in a pastoral plan should be limited to about five. If more than five major initiatives over a five-year period are identified, it is likely that resources will be spread over too many goals. The result could be that none of the goals are achieved at the level of quality needed by the community. The problem is not that the wrong goals were selected but that too many were. The concept of opportunity costs is crucial in such planning. The true cost of any goal is the goals that we forgo. We cannot do everything and thus must focus on doing a few things well. The issue is to identify the critical few goals that will make the most progress toward achieving the mission and moving toward the vision.

There are other more practical reasons for limiting the number of goals. It is difficult to keep our attention focused on even five major goals or initiatives. All of us have busy lives in which competition for our attention has increased exponentially. The fewer focal points we have, the more likely we can give the quality and quantity of attention required.

Of course, the other reason is that we never start from scratch. While it sounds nice and productive to talk about zero-based budgeting and planning, we never start from zero. There are people, programs, and buildings already in place and needing attention. If we are lucky, we may have 20 percent of our resources available for redeployment into new initiatives. Thus it is essential that we choose the vital few rather than the comprehensive, but often trivial, many.

Sample Goals

1. By (month & year), the community will gather as one at a single Sunday Eucharist each week.

2. By (month & year), 50 percent of the parish will be participating in small group faith sharing.
3. By (month & year), every member will be actively involved in a life of stewardship.

Objectives

Objectives are activities, typically extending over a multi-year time period, that are required to achieve the goals of the pastoral plan. The most important question about an objective is whether or not it is an effective and efficient means to achieve the goal. The practical judgment of those who will be responsible for implementing an objective is essential to the articulation of it. This often requires an effective interface between staff and members of the pastoral council or whatever team is doing the planning.

Objectives have definite time frames, expected results, and defined responsibilities. Again, care should be exercised in not establishing too many objectives for any goal. Everything worthwhile cannot be done at once. Realistic appraisal of costs of all types is essential along with realistic timeframes and expectations.

Objectives include . . .

1. an action verb,
2. a specific task to be completed,
3. a target group,
4. assigned responsibility, and
5. a completion date.

Sample Objectives for Goal # 3 above: by (month & year), every member will be actively involved in a life of stewardship.

1. During year one, pastoral leader will identify, recruit, and form a stewardship team for the community.
2. During year one, the stewardship team will organize for a comprehensive stewardship process.
3. During year two, the stewardship team will conduct an educational process for the faith community.
4. During year three, the stewardship team and staff will conduct a pilot test of the stewardship process.
5. During year four, the stewardship team and staff will begin a three-year process of full implementation of a communitywide stewardship process.

Annual Action Steps

Annual action steps are the specific tasks to be undertaken in any year to achieve an objective that, in turn, achieves a goal. The goals, taken together over a five-year period, advance the community toward its vision. Action steps are developed each year and need to be integrated into an annual operating plan and budget. As the process moves from goals to objectives to action steps, it is essential that those responsible for the implementation be involved directly. Nothing can be worse than a plan developed by well meaning but relatively uninformed people who then present it to volunteers or staff for immediate implementation.

The following chart displays sample annual action steps for the first objective.

	Sep	Oct	Nov	Dec	Jan	Feb	Mar	Apr	May
Gather names of potential members from pastoral council and staff	*	*							
Meet with potential members to inform			*						
Meet for discernment				*					
Affirm decisions					*				
Announce to community						*			

Involvement of Major Groups in Key Planning Elements

Within a faith community at all three levels (parish, diocese, and region), there are at least six groups of people who are involved in pastoral planning. Each group has a role that often varies depending on the planning element under consideration.

The following reviews the role of each group.

Chart available at avemariapress.com

Element	Pastoral Leader	Pastoral Council	Planning Team	Community	Staff	Lay Ministry Leaders
Mission	leadership	leadership	active & direct	reactive input	reactive input	reactive input
Vision	leadership	leadership	active & direct	reactive input	reactive input	reactive input
Goals	leadership	leadership	active & direct	reactive input	active direct/ reactive input	active direct/ reactive input
Objectives	leadership	reactive input	active & direct	reactive input	active direct	active direct
Action Steps	leadership	reactive input	active & direct	reactive input	active direct	active direct

PASTORAL LEADER

For every faith community, there is a person or team authorized to serve as the pastoral leader. Depending on the type of community, this leader could be a pastor, a pastoral administrator/parish life coordinator, a bishop, a vicar, or a team of people as described in canon 517§2. This person or team is responsible for providing effective leadership at all levels and for the development of all key components of the plan. The type of leadership required is one that empowers those involved in the process in authentic ways, while at the same time appropriately expressing the authority invested in the pastoral leadership position. In the end, any pastoral leader should manage him- or herself in a way that facilitates the members of the community taking their proper role in the process so that the results truly represent the action of the Spirit in the community rather than the authority, no matter how legitimate, of the formal leader. The pastoral leader also assumes a more active role in the development of objectives and action steps since these begin to move into managing

A Concise Guide to Pastoral Planning

the implementation of the plan. The pastoral leader's role is to make sure that the plans developed by the planning team, staff, and lay ministry leaders are realistic and consistent with the overall operation of the faith community.

PASTORAL COUNCIL

The Pastoral Council participates with the pastoral leader in providing empowering leadership to the development of mission, vision, and goals. The council also plays a special role in affirming the results of the process and recommending them to the pastoral leader. The role of the council begins to shift as the process moves to objectives and action steps. The council, along with the community, moves to a more reactive role. This results from the movement toward implementation and the necessity for those closest to the work to assume a more active role in the development of plans.

PLANNING TEAM

In many cases, the pastoral council will gather a planning team to develop a pastoral plan for the council's review and affirmation. If this is not the case, the council will sometimes sit as the pastoral council and sometimes as the planning team. The planning team plays an active and direct role in all five key components of the pastoral plan. Even though it does not make the final affirmation of the plan, it must do the work and arrange for others to do the work required for each component. In the development of objectives and action steps, this requires an effective partnership with staff and lay ministry leaders, often working through special joint teams for each goal and objective. It is essential that the planning team manage the development of objectives and action steps in a way that directly and substantively involves staff and lay ministry leaders.

FAITH COMMUNITY

Members of the faith community must be engaged in all five key planning elements, but their involvement is one of reactive input. There are practical reasons for this. First, pastoral planning takes time, and all members of the community do not have the time available to devote to the planning process. Through its pastoral council and often then through a planning team, the community empowers some of their number to serve the community in this fashion. Nonetheless it is essential that the entire community be informed and involved appropriately. Input is required for all five elements. Other than in very small communities, community affirmation should take place through the ordinary process of community discernment, namely, through the pastoral council, rather than through community town hall meetings.

STAFF

In addition to the pastoral leader, most parishes today have lay ecclesial ministers (in full- or part-time service) and perhaps deacons. Along with the administrative staff (business managers, plant managers, and clerical support staff), the pastoral staff provides the ongoing programmatic or operational management of the parish. Together they support and empower ministry leaders and workers from within the community. In mission, vision, and goals, the pastoral staff should play a role consistent with their membership in the community, one of reactive input. Often, staff members have information and knowledge that the pastoral council or planning team will find valuable. Often, the planning team includes a staff member. But it is important that staff understand that they have no more authority in the development of mission, vision, and goals than do other members of the community. Their input should be obtained, perhaps in a specially designed process, along with the input from the community at large.

With objectives and action steps, the pastoral staff takes on a more important role consistent with their involvement in the work of the community. The planning team will look to the staff to develop objectives and action steps that will accomplish the goals confirmed by the pastoral council. In addition to their many other assets, the staff constitutes the program and ministry experts for a community, and they should be actively and directly involved in objectives and action steps. This shift begins with the development of goals. The staff begins to shift out of its reactive input role and into the active, direct role. The management of this transition is important to the success of the process: effectively engaging staff in a new role and keeping planning team members engaged as the team begins to share its role. The pastoral leader should be particularly alert to any signs that the pastoral staff feels devalued and alienated by their more reactive role in the early stages and should take steps to ensure their proper understanding of their role.

MINISTRY LEADERS

In some smaller faith communities, there may be no professional staff other than the pastor, parish administrator, or parish life coordinator. Members of the community provide the leadership and active involvement that in larger parishes is provided by staff. In larger communities with professional staff, however, members of the community are typically involved in the leadership of various ministries. In fact, the role of staff is often not to do the work of various ministries but to train, support, and nurture members of the community in that ministry work. In either case, the role of lay ministry leaders in the five pastoral planning elements mirrors that of the staff. It begins with reactive input for mission and vision, shifts to a blended reactive input/active and direct role in goals, and ends with an active, direct role in objectives and action steps.

Conclusion

These are the key elements of a pastoral plan. The process described in the next four chapters is designed to produce workable and effective materials that result in a mission statement, a vision statement, goals, objectives, and action steps. All of these are focused on a few vital activities out of all the activities of a community in order to make an impact on the direction of the community. The following chart is a handy reminder of the material covered in this chapter.

Chart available at avemariapress.com

Element	Brief Description	Timeframe	Key Questions	Number
Mission Statement	The purpose of the faith community: what it does, how it does it, and what difference it makes	Relatively stable over many years	1. Is it still vital for the community? 2. Do members know it and use it?	One
Vision Statement	What the future will be like if the mission is fully or more fully achieved; stated in present tense	Likely to be changed in a ten-year period and certainly with any change in leadership	1. Is it compelling for members? 2. Does it speak to both head and heart?	One
Goals	The major initiatives required to move toward the vision; investment of discretionary resources with some reallocation	Five years	1. Is this the next best step toward the vision? 2. Who is accountable?	No more than five
Objectives	The major activities required to achieve goals	Multi-year but no more than five	1. Are these efficient and effective means to achieve goal? 2. Who is accountable?	Three to five per goal
Action Steps	What needs to be done each year to meet the objectives and thus achieve the goals	Annual	1. What needs to be done next year to advance the objective? 2. Who is accountable?	Varies

The following graphic provides an overview of the five elements of pastoral planning and their relationship.

Chart available at avemariapress.com

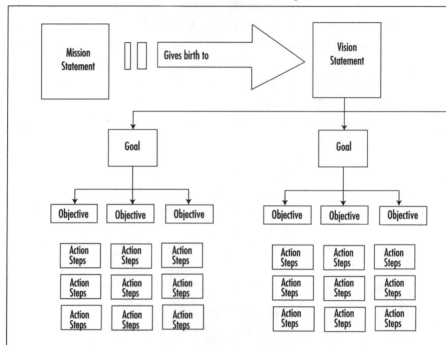

A Mission Statement gives birth to a Vision Statement, which describes a future state in which the mission is more fully fulfilled. Goals are major initiatives calculated over the next five years to move the faith community toward the envisioned future. Each goal has a limited number of objectives that will help the community achieve that goal. Each objective has a set of annual action steps required to achieve the objective. It is important to establish no more than three to five goals and to similarly limit objectives and action steps; otherwise the necessary activities will overwhelm a system already strained to meet its ordinary demands. Path of development is from mission down to action steps.

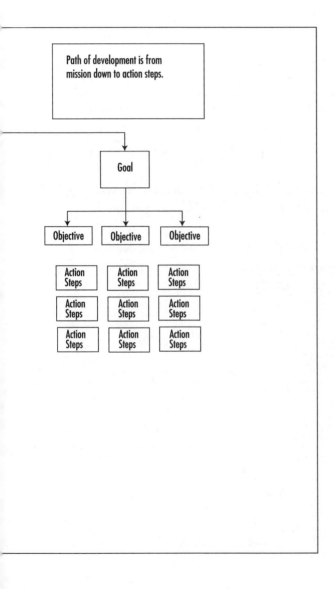

Study Questions

1. Without referring to a written source, write out the mission statement of your parish as you recall it or as you think it should be. Compare and contrast that with the actual mission statement if one exists.
2. Describe a time in your personal life when you had to think anew about your fundamental values or what Chris Argyris calls "double loop learning." Are the results of that learning still with you today?
3. When you plan for the future, do you tend to do a good job of estimating the time and effort involved? If not, do you underestimate or overestimate? What are the reasons for not estimating correctly, and what might be done about them?
4. In your parish or faith community, what are the major groups that should be involved in pastoral planning? Are the relationships between these clear?

CHAPTER 4

The Pastoral Planning Cycle

In this chapter we will explore a pastoral planning cycle beginning with the development of a mission statement, proceeding through an implementation plan, and concluding with an assessment process. We will build on the key elements of a pastoral plan described in chapter 3 and will use the definitions and insights of chapters 1 and 2. This generic process will be applied to the three significant levels of faith communities in the following three chapters. In this chapter we will be using the term "faith community." A faith community can be a diocese, a parish, a specialized ministry, or a regional grouping of parishes. As we saw in chapter 1, it is a faith community that provides the foundation for vitality at any level of the church. Using it here will help us focus on the general process. We will also use another convention in describing the body doing the work of pastoral planning. Since the names differ at various levels and since a pastoral council might well designate a planning team to do the hands-on planning work, we will use "planning team" as a generic term. In the following chapters, we will particularize this term to the three levels of planning.

The best pastoral planning processes are information-based, highly involving, flexible, committed to communication, collaborative, and realistic. The following graphic shows a complete pastoral planning cycle and the flow of activities and inter-relationships that will meet these criteria of effectiveness. In the following sections we will focus on each of the steps in sequence.

Pastoral Planning Cycle

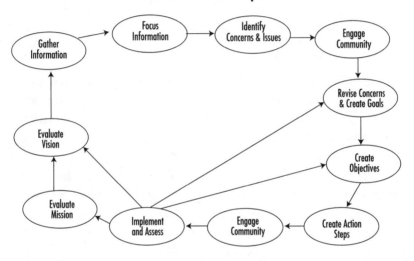

Chart available at avemariapress.com

The Mission Statement

Every planning process begins with the mission statement: a description of an organization's reason for being: the work it does, how it is done, and why it is important. A mission statement should be an idiosyncratic, compelling, and passionate statement of why the faith community exists. In other words, what is at stake in the flourishing of this particular faith community?

If the faith community already has a mission statement, the planning process begins by assessing its currency and potency and thus determining if a new mission statement is required. If there is no mission statement or if the current one is no longer useful, a full mission statement development process should be undertaken.

REVIEWING AN EXISTING MISSION STATEMENT

The planning team should assess a current mission statement by answering a set of questions designed to probe the relevance and vibrancy of the mission statement. The questions in the sample Mission Evaluation Sheet below are illustrative, not exhaustive. Each planning team should add, subtract, and change the questions in order to tailor to its specific situation.

Sample Mission Evaluation Sheet (Chart available at avemariapress.com)	
After reviewing the attached mission statement, place yourself in a prayerful state by recalling your gratefulness to God for the gift of life, perhaps by reading and reflecting on *Suscipe*, a prayer of St. Ignatius. (See Resources Appendix A.) Then proceed to answer each question based on your knowledge and experience. No answer is right or wrong— just make sure it is yours. Do not complete the rating portion. This will be explained at our planning team meeting. Once you have completed the form, send a copy to the chair of the planning team, who will distribute copies of all responses to all members in preparation for our meeting.	
Question	**Rating**
How long ago was the mission statement developed? Have the circumstances of the faith community changed appreciably since then? If yes, in what ways?	
Is the mission statement clearly a mission statement of this particular faith community? Or is it a generic statement that could easily apply to any faith community? Cite examples.	
Does the mission statement continue to be used in both written and verbal communication? If yes, give examples.	
When discussions of pastoral priorities and ministries take place, is the mission statement referred to as a basis for decision and choice? If yes, give examples.	
Do the people of the faith community know the mission statement and use its language to describe their community? If yes, give examples. If no, why not?	
Has there been a change in leadership of the faith community since the mission statement was developed? If yes, how would you characterize the differences in leadership?	
Has the membership of the community changed appreciably since the mission statement was developed? If yes, in what ways?	
Based on your thoughtful and prayerful review and your answers to the above questions, what do you think about the current mission statement?	
Do not feel constrained by the above boxes. If you need more space, add sheets.	

Each member of the planning team should complete a mission evaluation worksheet and share responses with the rest of the members before the team meets to assess the mission statement. At the assessment meeting, the leader should facilitate an open discussion of each question and seek to develop a consensus within the group. It is certainly not necessary and actually ill-advised to take votes in this process. If there are those who answer the questions differently than others, it is because they have different perspectives or perhaps different understandings than others do. These perspectives need to be shared with the entire team so that everyone moves ahead with the same information.

At the conclusion of the discussion, the facilitator invites each member to indicate whether a new or revised mission statement is needed. Using their own initial responses, those from other members, and the team discussion, members complete the rating section using the following directions from the facilitator.

> Recalling your initial responses to each question, and reflecting on the responses of other team members within our discussion, indicate how you feel about the mission statement using a rating from 1 to 5, with 5 = No reason to revise or rewrite the mission statement, 3 = Revise current mission statement but not a complete rewrite, and 1 = Definitely develop a new mission statement. Give a rating based on each question and then finally indicate an overall rating.

The facilitator collects the totals and then summarizes the completed forms. Using a blank rating sheet printed on poster-sized paper, an overhead projector transparency, or an LCD-projected document, the facilitator shows the results to the team. Individual ratings are tallied within the response box, with the average shown in the rating box. This provides the team with an overall rating as well as a way of seeing dispersion in the ratings. Outlying ratings invite input from those raters to help the team gain a more complete understanding. If there is not a clear consensus, the team continues to discuss and share until a direction is clear. Eventually the direction becomes clear: use the existing mission statement, revise the statement, or write a new one.

REVISING AN EXISTING MISSION STATEMENT

Sometimes the planning team thinks the current mission statement has enough relevance and power to continue to be a statement of purpose and intention. However, the team concludes that enough had changed in the circumstances of the community to require revision, probably in some specific ways. The directions and ideas of revisions emerge from the group process of answering the evaluation questions. The planning team should use a writing team to facilitate the writing of the mission statement. This is an approach that will be used often in this pastoral planning cycle.

A small group, typically no more than three, accepts the responsibility for translating the thoughts of the team into specific written language for the planning team's consideration, modification, and affirmation. In this and in other uses of a writing team, the team does not so much write the mission statement as it serves as staff to the planning team by providing concrete language for consideration. This avoids one of the major pitfalls of larger committees: the attempt to write a document with too many people involved.

This is a repetitive process in which the writing team develops drafts, obtains feedback from the planning team, revises drafts, receives more feedback, and so on until the text reflects the views of the planning team. The chair of the writing team must provide leadership here. The objective is not simply to list what everyone says and figure out how to include his or her exact words. Rather it is to understand the thoughts and desires of the planning team and then enflesh them in words and phrases.

CREATING A NEW MISSION STATEMENT

If the team decides that the current mission statement is no longer useful for planning purposes or if there is no mission statement at all, the team begins a process of developing and affirming a mission statement. If the team has assessed a mission statement using the given questions, it can use those assessments in the development process. However, the team must focus directly on the mission development itself.

There are two essential elements to an effective process: good questions and engagement. The questions used to generate responses for the construction of a mission statement should be ones to which people do not have stock answers. Catechism-type answers to questions of purpose will result only in generic responses and a premature closure of discussion because the "right" answers have been given.

The second element is engagement. If the process of developing a mission statement effectively involves and engages members of the community, the process itself may be as important as the exact content of the statement itself. The process of developing a mission statement can be a shared experience out of which a deeper sense of community emerges. Out of that deeper sense of community comes a more compelling mission. The development of a mission statement can be an important opportunity of deepening the sense of the faith community as the communion of disciples and as the living Body of Christ.

The team begins with each member completing a Mission Development Worksheet, shown next.

Sample Mission Development Worksheet (Chart at avemariapress.com)
(1) Take a few moments to calm yourself and disconnect from the pressing concerns of your life. Perhaps the gospel reading for the day and prayerfully reflecting on its meaning for you will be helpful. (2) Then turn attention to the questions on the sheet. The first one asks you to construct a mission statement for our faith community using a set format that has proven useful with other communities. Complete that as best you can. It may take more than one session. Don't hesitate to set it aside after you have jotted down some ideas, and then come back to it later. Also don't hesitate to try out your formulation on friends, your spouse, or children. (3) After you complete this first response, review the remaining questions and jot down your answers. (4) Finally, review the answers to those last questions, and then go back to your mission formulation to see if you would make any changes. (5) Pray often in the process. We are about spiritual work, that is, work that the Spirit does in and through us. Provide time and space for that.
This first question can lead to fruitful discussions about the three elements of a mission statement: the core work of the community, the unique way in which it approaches its work, and what happens as a result. Complete the following sentence: our faith community does something (<u>the core work of the community</u>) in such a way that (<u>the unique approach to work</u>) so that (<u>the result</u>) happens.
Why do people belong to this faith community? What do they seek to achieve for themselves, for others, and for the community by being members?
If you had to describe the faith community in one word, what would it be?
If you had to describe the faith community in one sentence, what would it be?
If the faith community didn't exist, what would be missing from the Church or the wider community?
If Jesus were here today, to what would he call this faith community? How would he ask each member and the community as a whole to be his disciples?

The answers to these questions can lead to fruitful discussions about a mission statement. A good group process can facilitate a consensus around these three elements embedded in the first question. The other questions provide additional information about the nature of the faith community and its current reality. Using a writing team, the planning team develops a series of drafts of the mission statement based on the individual answers to the mission question. Obviously there is no single set of correct questions. Each team should develop its own set using those provided here as starting points. Each member writes out his or her own answers to these questions and provides copies to all members of the team. The team meets to review and discuss the answers with a particular eye to identifying patterns in the responses. This may take more than a single meeting. Structured brainstorming is an effective method for beginning this process. One or more grouping techniques can be used to categorize responses. Nominal group voting techniques can also be used to identify those items that appear relatively more important to the team. (These and other well-proven group techniques are available for download at avemariapress.com)

The writing team can then begin its work by developing at least two, but not more than three, draft mission statements. The writing team provides these drafts to the planning team in advance of a meeting. At the meeting, the members of the writing team take careful notes of what is said about the strengths and weaknesses of the statements, which thoughts and phrases seem to resonate, which directions seem promising, and which seem of little interest. The planning team need not arrive at a consensus at this meeting unless a strong consensus does, in fact, develop. The writing team takes this input from the meeting and revises the draft statements, perhaps moving to one or two versions.

The focus of the next meeting is to arrive at a workable consensus that a draft is "good enough" to present to the larger community to obtain its input and reaction. In fact, it is important that the draft not be perfect and final. If there are two different drafts, so much the better. If the planning team asks the community to respond to a statement that seems final and without options, community members tend to not respond and to think that the decisions have already been made. This is not a good way to start a pastoral planning process! Chapter 8, on communication, describes many ways to obtain this community feedback.

Once the team hears from the community, it works with its writing team to revise and finalize the mission statement. It then either recommends the mission statement to the pastoral council or—acting in its capacity as a pastoral council—it affirms the mission statement. Along with the pastoral leader, the pastoral council promulgates the mission statement to the faith community. From this point in the planning process, the mission statement is the standard by which the team judges options and possibilities.

The Vision Statement

While the mission statement helps us understand who a faith community is, what it does, how it exists, and what difference it makes, a vision statement helps us understand where it is headed: what future state embodies the fuller accomplishment of the mission statement. Every vision statement implies a change in behavior in order to move from the current reality toward a future of fuller life and effectiveness.

The planning team uses a similar technique to the one used for a mission statement. Taking a future time period, often ten years in the future, members complete a vision worksheet as show next.

Sample Vision Statement Worksheet (Chart available at avemariapress.com)
Prayerfully prepare yourself to reflect on these questions by reading the Psalm responses for today's Mass. Reflect on how God is speaking to you through that Psalm. In a quiet place with at least thirty minutes to spend, begin to answer these questions as part of developing a vision statement for the community. You may find it helpful to do this in two or more sessions. Don't hesitate to share your work with friends or family and listen carefully to their reactions.
Describe the everyday reality of our faith community if we were to fully accomplish our mission. What would we be doing, saying, building, changing, etc.?
How would others describe us if we were to fully accomplish our mission?
What would you have the faith community do if we were to be bold in seeking to accomplish our mission?
If we didn't care how others would view us, what would we do to achieve our mission?
If we could do only one thing to accomplish our mission, what would that be and how would it change the faith community in the future?

Each member answers these questions and any others that the team might develop. They are provided to the team in advance of a meeting to review. From that point on, the process would mirror that used with the mission statement: interactive drafts, one or two options good enough for review, reaction from the community, revision, and final affirmation and promulgation.

Assessing Where We Are / Gathering Information

With mission and vision statements in hand, the planning team now moves into a more analytical phase of the planning process. Since we tend to come to planning efforts thinking we know what needs to be done, it is important to take a step back, look at information about how things really are, and re-understand the current situation with the problems and opportunities contained therein. In some ways, it is important to almost overwhelm ourselves with information so we are forced to arrive at our conclusions anew. Perhaps our conclusions do not change, but it is important that we go through a process of analysis using current information.

While the extent and complexity of the data will vary, there are four types of information to include at the beginning of the planning process:

- internal community demographics,
- external community demographics,
- assessments of key pastoral areas, and
- policy constraints.

The specific information will vary among the three levels of pastoral planning. Chapters 5, 6, and 7 contain appropriate specifics.

INTERNAL DEMOGRAPHICS

Information should be displayed over a long enough time horizon, five years, so that trends are apparent. Single data points, no matter how accurate, are not as helpful as a time series of data points. It is also important to be able to compare and contrast information across different categories of communities. Comparing the information describing one community to a national average may be meaningless, whereas comparing it to a peer group of similarly situated communities may be very helpful and certainly more realistic. The following is an example of the type of information that would be of benefit and the various comparison subgroups.

1. Mass attendance report
   a. Number of Sunday obligation Masses
   b. Average Weekend Attendance by Mass
   c. Capacity of Worship Space
   d. Average Capacity Used
2. Sacramental report
   a. Number of baptisms
      i. Infants
      ii. Children (RCIC)
      iii. Adults (RCIA)
   b. Number of full membership
   c. Confirmations
   d. Weddings
   e. Funerals
3. Number of participants in:
   a. Religious education
   b. Youth ministry
   c. Catholic school
   d. Adult education
4. Demographics
   a. Registered households
   b. Map showing locations of registered households
   c. Registered members (individuals)
   d. Age distribution of registered members
   e. Number of baptized Catholics
   f. Race and ethnic profiles
   g. Newly registered members
   h. Widowed, divorced members
5. Financial
   a. Ordinary income per registered household
   b. Total income
   c. Catholic school expense
   d. Staff salaries and benefits including relationship to diocesan standards

     e. Faith community tithing
     f. Total expense
     g. Net revenue
     h. Number of envelope users and percent of
         total households
6. Facilities
     a. Number and condition of facilities
     b. Urgent capital needs/issues

Each community will develop its own particular set of information needs. Many will develop quite elaborate reports, while others will focus on a few key statistics.

EXTERNAL DEMOGRAPHICS

Information about those already related to the faith community is clearly important, but equally important is information about those within the sphere of concern of the community but not formally associated with it. There are numerous sources of such information that can become quite complex. Often people in the community are either expert at understanding and communicating such information or have relationships with local planning agencies or universities who can make such expertise available. Most of this information, though not all, comes from the federal census and its updates.

Basic demographic information—counts and categories—is available online at www.census.gov. This site provides basic census information, in many cases down to the census tract and block. It is most easily available through the American Fact Finder feature of the site available at www.factfinder.census.gov/servlet/BasicFactsServlet. This is a relatively easy-to-use service that can provide a great deal of useful information. It does take some time to become comfortable with census information and how to extract and display it. Local planning and social service agencies are particularly good sources for information about people who are economically or socially vulnerable: elderly, young, sick, poor, unemployed or underemployed, institutionalized, handicapped, etc. Local school districts have a great deal of information on young people within their service area, including social, economic, and educational issues. These agencies are typically very interested in helping local groups assess their role in the community.

Vendors of demographic and other information also exist. These organizations take basic demographic data, in some cases add to it, and increase the value of the data by turning it into useful information, displayed in a more easily understood format. One of the leading firms of this type is Percept. Its website is a helpful summary of their services and is available at www.perceptgroup.com Percept is especially important for pastoral planning because it is the only national vendor of demographic information that is specifically and solely focused on churches and faith communities. Percept's mission statement says it well: To provide the best information-based planning tools to churches, regional bodies, and other religious organizations in the United States.

Perhaps of most interest to a faith community that wants to look at census and other information about its service area is a Percept product called Ministry Area Profile (MAP). A wealth of information is provided for a geographic area delineated by the user. Since the system accepts polygons, it is suited to the boundaries of a typical Catholic faith community. The resulting report is information-rich and presented in a graphic-oriented, user-friendly format. In addition to Census information, the MAP also includes population projections and information from Percept's own Ethos database using lifestyle analysis and ongoing surveys of religious behavior and attitudes. This extensive snapshot is available from the Percept website for a very reasonable price. For the amount of information and the usefulness of its presentation, this is a very cost-effective way to provide this kind of information.

EVALUATING KEY AREAS OF PASTORAL CONCERN

In addition to the quantitative information described above, the information gathering phase needs to focus on the activity and life in the essential areas of pastoral life. In chapter 2 we looked at the five dimensions of pastoral life:

1. Word
2. Worship
3. Community
4. Service
5. Temporalities

Whatever schema is being used, there should be a thorough review and assessment of each area. Indicators of success or vitality descriptors are essential. They become the questions that are asked about each pastoral area. Those who are familiar with the area under consideration should conduct this assessment. For example, people familiar with a community's religious education should be asked to assess its effectiveness, that is, the extent to which there is evidence to support the validity of the descriptors. An illustrative set of these descriptors can be found in the chapters dealing with the specific planning levels.

The collection of this qualitative information must be guided by a set of questions arising from the indicators or descriptors. As this information is summarized and digested, a picture emerges of the life of the community in each of the pastoral areas. No attempt is made at this point to draw conclusions but only to ensure that information accurately reflects the experience in each of the pastoral areas. Specific sample questions for parishes, dioceses, and regional groups are included in chapters 5, 6, and 7, respectively.

ASSESSING GUIDELINES AND CONSTRAINTS

In addition to information about the community and those it serves, it is important to have information on policies and guidelines that may be relevant to the community and its planning. These policies can cover the gamut: human resources, sacramental guidelines, financial policies, regional structure, etc. Very often these policies and constraints come from other organizations at higher levels within the Church, from canon law (the universal law of the Church), civil law, or from the policies and values of the specific community. Again, there are examples in the specific applications in chapters 5, 6, and 7.

LOOKING AT OTHER SOURCES

No listing of information sources can be complete. Each community will have its own set of issues and its own way of collecting and processing information about its life. The emphasis at this point is to include other sources of information rather than prematurely limit them. As complete as any information might be, there are always issues and concerns that might not become known. Either as part of the assessment of key pastoral areas or in separately organized focus groups, leading questions about faith community life in general should be posed. Using focus group methodology can be very helpful in unearthing issues and concerns that do not fit neatly into any predetermined category. Chapter 8, dealing with communication, has information on how to conduct focus groups.

Focusing Information

With this mass of information, the challenge is to process it in such a way that the important insights and issues begin to stand out from background noise. There is no simple, linear process to accomplish this. It requires a more creative approach based on the members of the planning team becoming immersed in the data and information and answering two key questions in each area: What in this information gives me hope for the future? What in this information raises concerns or issues for the future? Each person will have his or her own perspective and will thus arrive at different answers to these questions.

It is important that these two questions be posed and answered in each of the information areas: internal community demographic information, external community demographic information, pastoral areas (each one treated as a separate area), and policies and constraints. Through a group process and consensus, the planning team will arrive at its summary conclusions based on its analysis of the information in each area. Obviously these summary conclusions will not cover anything close to the reality of these areas. They will, however, focus on strengths and accomplishments and on those areas in which the reality has fallen short of the community's mission and vision. The following form is useful to assist people in this process.

Sample Information Focus Form (Chart available at avemariapress.com)

Information Category: (e.g., Internal Community Demographics: Sacramental)

List the five facts or trends that strike you as the most significant in this area:

1.

2.

3.

4.

5.

What in this information gives me hope for the future?

What in this information raises concerns or issues for the future?

Identifying Concerns, Issues, and Ideals

Through brainstorming processes, the planning team begins to identify the concerns and issues raised by the assessment above. There is no simple, linear process to map from the conclusions to a statement of concerns and issues. This requires a more holistic approach. Once a consensus is reached on a draft set of concerns and issues, it is helpful to perform a force field analysis identifying forces that are moving the community in the direction of progress or solution and those that are impeding progress. This single sheet of paper is a succinct statement of the concern and presents the planning team's preliminary analysis of the issue. Below is a sample force field analysis completed for a potential pastoral issue.

Faith Community Major Issues Report	
Description of Issue/Concern The number and proportion of young adults (19-30) attending Mass and/or participating in parish life is declining and is now very low.	
Positive Forces	**Restraining Forces**
1. We have a welcoming liturgy. 2. We have young adults as leaders. 3. We are concerned. 4. Our programs are family-based. 5. We have good sacramental preparation.	1. Young adults have little time for sustained participation. 2. Our programs are family-based. 3. We have no staff with expertise in this area. 4. The full gospel church is attracting our young adults. 5. There is little economic opportunity here. 6. Preaching does not address issues of young adults.

In this process it is important to focus on concerns and not priorities. Any community has many priorities that consume most of its resources. However, a priority is not a concern unless members of the community feel that it is not being adequately addressed. For example, most people would identify the religious education of children as a priority of a parish, yet few will identify it as a concern because they typically feel that the parish is doing a good job of addressing this priority. On the other hand, the religious engagement of young adults is typically listed as a concern because people feel that this is not being well addressed or could be addressed at a substantially greater level of effectiveness. A well-addressed priority does not rise to the level of a concern and thus little dramatic change may be necessary. A priority without an effective response, however, demands change in the behavior of the community because it is not being well addressed. Resources will have to flow to this area and the methodology will have to change in order to get different results. It is not that one is a higher priority than the other, but rather that dramatic change is demanded in one and not the other.

Engaging the Faith Community

At this point, the planning team is ready to engage the entire faith community. Of course, it has been keeping the community informed of its work and has already engaged the community in the review and affirmation of mission and vision statements, but now it has some results to share with the community and to obtain its reaction. The method for doing this should be consistent with the style and culture of the faith community. Some faith communities use committees or other smaller venues. Some have little experience with bringing the entire community together to discuss important pastoral issues. The format of the force field analysis lends itself to newsletter or bulletin insert communication.

Many communities have a tradition of open community meetings to process such material. Sheets enlarged to poster size can be posted in the meeting area. As people circulate to view and discuss the issues, members of the planning team are stationed at the posters to answer questions and engage in discussion. It looks much like a poster session at a professional meeting. People are also encouraged to use available marker pens to make notations on the posters, including adding forces and adjusting language.

To assist in getting a sense of the community's reaction to the concerns and issues, some planning teams issue colored dots of sticky paper and encourage people to vote for the concern or issue they feel is the most important. They can spend their votes in any combination they would like. After the session, the members of the planning team have a good idea of where the life and enthusiasm of the parish is heading. This is especially helpful if the council has identified more issues than the recommended five. The "voting" by the community helps the planning team to "see" where the mind of the community is leaning. (See Chapter 8 for details about these techniques.)

Revising and Finalizing Issues & Opportunities

The planning team uses the results of this consultation with the community to revise these pastoral concerns and issues. Based on the assessment by members of the community and the judgment of the team members, the team reduces the issues to a manageable but critical few. During this process, the team always keeps the mission and vision in mind since they provide the overall sense of direction and meaning.

While the planning team listens carefully to the input and reaction from the community, it serves the faith community best when it exercises its own judgment. In much the same way that an elected representative operates, team members reflect the views and judgments of community members but do so through the lens of their own experience and knowledge. Team members have spent time becoming informed about the needs and issues that confront the community. They have gone through extensive information-gathering in the initial phase of pastoral planning. It is up to them to bring all of these sources of information together in order to make choices that will release the energy of the community.

All the concerns and issues raised by the process are important and significant to the life of the community; otherwise they would not have arisen from the process. This point in the process is not about eliminating some and keeping others, but rather about deciding which ones will be those that the community focuses on for the next three to five years. Nothing is lost, but some issues will be addressed first and others later. The council will use good group process to arrive at a consensus about the vital few concerns and issues that will be the subject of the rest of the planning process.

In selecting those vital few, the council will obviously focus on those that appear to be the most important and significant. However, it should also factor in the degree of difficulty of responding to an issue. Any list should include very important and hard-to-solve concerns, as well as some that are perhaps somewhat less important but admit of easier solution. The best situation is to find very important and easy-to-solve concerns, the "low-hanging fruit." Early success in implementation is important to the continuation of effective pastoral planning.

Developing Goals

Once the planning team identifies the vital few concerns, it formats them as goals if this has not already been done. There is an advantage in using the concern format along with the force field analysis because it tends to keep options open and encourages input and reaction. As the planning moves forward, however, it is necessary to reshape the material into the goal format discussed in the goal section above.

Once the major issues have been developed into goals, these should be communicated to the community. It will be important to point out that the goals identified in this process do not typically include everything that a community does, but rather those areas in which it wants to invest its discretionary energy to bring about change. There are many very important and significant areas of community life that will not necessarily be included in this focused planning.

Articulating Objectives and Action Plans

For each goal, the council should develop a set of action plans, composed of objectives and related action steps. Using the methodology discussed above, a workable set of actions should be devised that will move the community closer to the state envisioned by the goal and thus closer to a fulfillment of its mission, its reason for being. Since a goal looks at a three- to five-year planning horizon, the objectives should be staged over the same horizon. Those objectives that will happen over the next year should have sufficient details as indicated next. Those that will take place beyond the next year do not need that level of detail but should be included to situate the next year's activities within the context of the entire process. Unless it is very simple and easy to achieve, any goal requires more than one year of change to achieve.

As the council moves toward objectives and action plans, it will begin to deal with the practical realities of achieving its goals. No planning process can successfully focus on the entire life of an organization. There are so many demands on a community that 80 percent of its resources are devoted to the maintenance of ongoing activities. If it is lucky, it has discretion over 20 percent of its time, talent, and treasure. It is this 20 percent that can be devoted to change and transformation. However, this 20 percent is not easily available because it is also being used to support ongoing activities. A planning process that focuses on change requires a reallocation of resources from ongoing activities to change activities. A careful estimate of the nature, extent, and timing of needed resources is essential to successful implementation. This planning must be coordinated with the ongoing budget planning of the community so that resources become available to support objectives and action plans. This is especially important if the community is complex with a highly developed program and professional staff.

The most overlooked resource is not money, but people's time. It is all too easy to come up with new initiatives to achieve important goals without realizing the impact on both staff and volunteer time. Merely to state that new activity will take place without providing for the additional or reallocated resources necessary can be irresponsible. In a time when pastoral leaders note the increasing difficulty of attracting volunteers to community activities, a plan that calls for additional volunteer or staff time must address ways in which that will happen.

Each community will have its own way of assessing the practical and budget impacts of new initiatives, but the following list is minimum set of requirements in an action step planning form:

Sample Action Step Planning Form (Chart available at avemariapress.com)
Clear description of the planned action:
Who will be responsible for implementation?
What is the timing of implementation?
What are the detectable results of successful implementation?

What resources are required?
    1. Staff time
    2. Volunteer time
    3. Materials
    4. Program support
    5. Outside resources
    6. Space
    7. Other

What are the sources for these resources?
What is the timing and method for evaluation?

Engaging the Faith Community

Once the entire plan is assembled but well before it is implemented, the planning team presents the plan to the entire community for its reaction and input. There are a variety of methods for this process. Because of the amount of material being presented, however, the team should consider the use of an executive summary of no more than three pages, along with making the entire draft plan available on demand, perhaps on the community web page. Members of the community are invited to make comments. The planning team is especially interested in learning if the community members see the plan as reflecting the values and concerns of the community, being consistent with and supportive of the community's mission and vision, and constituting a reasonable response to the issues and concerns raised by the planning process.

Implementing and Assessing

The result of this planning is a reaffirmed or new mission statement, vision statement, three to five change goals, a set of objectives, and action steps to achieve these goals over the next three to five years. The objectives are organized by goals but can also be shown by staff area, time period, pastoral area, or any other category that is meaningful to a specific audience. The one-year action steps are developed in sufficient detail to be included in the community operating plan, with longer term objectives stated but not fully developed. These will be elaborated and adjusted as part of the annual assessment and updating.

Conclusion

This chapter has reviewed the major components of a pastoral planning process, demonstrated their inter-relationship, and provided tools to assist in its implementation. While the process here has been generic, the next three chapters apply this process to the particular situations of parishes, dioceses, and regional groupings of parishes.

Study Questions

1. Modify the sample mission evaluation and creation worksheets to fit your parish or faith community. How do these seem to fit your faith community?
2. These processes are based on developing a consensus rather than voting. In what ways does this seem workable to you? What are the challenges and pitfalls in this approach? How might these challenges be dealt with and the pitfalls avoided?
3. Does your pastoral council routinely deal with the information described in this chapter? What will be the challenges in gathering and using this and similar information?
4. What schema for the key pastoral areas does your diocese use? If you are not aware of them, how would you go about finding out?
5. Does it make sense to you that pastoral planning should be an ongoing activity? What are the advantages and disadvantages of it being so?

CHAPTER 5

Implementation at the Parish Level

In this chapter we will consider how the pastoral planning process described in chapter 4 applies to an individual parish or faith community. The following two chapters will discuss application at the diocesan and the regional levels. Throughout this chapter we will be using "parishes" to designate any local faith community of Catholics drawn together in a stable manner and regularly celebrating Eucharist. This description includes not only parishes but also campus ministries, prison ministries, and many health care ministries. We also include ministries that serve special groups of disciples (for example, migrant workers, ethnic groups, or immigrant groups) even though they have not been established as canonical parishes. Wherever a stable community forms around the Eucharist, it can use the process described here for pastoral planning. Our shorthand for these communities will be "parishes" even if some of them do not meet the canonical requirements for parishes.

We will not repeat material fully developed in chapter 4, but will focus on issues specific to parishes and on the aspects of the process that need to be particularized for use by parishes. In this chapter we will look at organizational issues, methods for successful initiation of a parish pastoral planning process, some pastoral planning cycle issues specific to parishes, and relationships to parish groups and staff.

Organizational Issues

Pastoral planning begins with the pastor or pastoral leader. No planning process can achieve its full potential without the active support and encouragement of the person named by the bishop to provide leadership to the community. The pastoral leader works closely with the pastoral staff, lay ministry leaders, and community leaders to unearth the need for pastoral planning, to understand the nature of pastoral planning and to determine what it is and how it will be done. At the very beginning, leadership faces a key decision about how to organize for planning. There are two options: the parish pastoral council or a planning team empowered by the pastoral council. There is no one right way; each has advantages and disadvantages. We take as a given that there is a parish pastoral council. If one does not exist, pastoral leadership should deal with this issue before attempting the pastoral planning envisioned here. A properly constituted (according to canon law) and formed pastoral council operating at moderate levels of effectiveness is the sine qua non of pastoral planning.

PARISH PASTORAL COUNCIL

As we have seen in chapter 1, a pastoral council is a group broadly representative of the parish community that investigates and ponders significant pastoral issues and develops creative and effective responses to those issues. It reads the signs of the times and devises the actions of the faith community, the Body of Christ, to respond to the discerned pastoral issues and needs. Since this is the essence of pastoral planning, it seems obvious that a pastoral council should be the lead group in carrying out that planning. However, there are advantages and disadvantages to this obvious approach.

A. ADVANTAGES

A fully functioning pastoral council is already in place and thus planning can begin more quickly without the necessity of recruitment and formation of a planning team. A properly formed pastoral council will easily understand pastoral planning as described here. Importantly, it will proceed from a solid spiritual base since it will be using prayer and faith sharing as part of its normal council routines. On the other hand, if an existing parish pastoral council needs to be re-formed as a true pastoral council, the planning process can be an opportunity to do that. While this might somewhat delay the beginning of the planning process, it will yield long-term benefits to the parish. A parish and leadership committed to true pastoral planning may well find pastoral planning the opportunity to re-found and refocus the pastoral council away from a purely administrative approach.

There are also some practical advantages to using the pastoral council to do the direct work of pastoral planning. An existing pastoral council is typically a reservoir of the history of the parish. The members either know how things have come to be the way they are or know people who know. They typically have good working relationships with the pastoral staff and the lay ministry leaders. Unless there are significant dysfunctions, a pastoral council has significant advantages in taking the active lead role in planning.

B. DISADVANTAGES

There are, however, some disadvantages with a pastoral council. As a group, a council is already in place with a set of expectations for its work. This often does not include pastoral planning, so a significant change in behavior and relationships may be required. Further, an existing pastoral council may not have the quantity and quality of human resources needed for pastoral planning. Of course, all members are focused on the good of the parish, and they bring diverse skills and abilities, but there may also be some significant gaps in knowledge and skills. Given the nature of discernment or appointment of members and the way in which they are selected, it may not be possible or practical to change members or add those needed for the planning task without causing some significant negative side effects.

Old habits die hard. It is always tempting for an existing council to allow inertia to rule the day and to continue business as usual rather than invest the time and energy required for true system change. Pastoral councils are often consumed by the coordination of ministries in the parish, the coordination of community building and/or fund raising events, and a meeting agenda that spends most of its time hearing committee reports rather than engaging in challenging discussions about the action of the Body of Christ here and now. It may be wise to create a special planning team rather than trying to change these habits quickly.

PASTORAL PLANNING TEAM

The other option is to appoint a special planning team to conduct the work of pastoral planning. While there may be times when it is necessary to proceed to pastoral planning without a pastoral council, this should be avoided if at all possible. Pastoral planning is the true work of a pastoral council, and pastoral leaders should not confuse an already murky situation by using a planning team independently of a pastoral council.

However, there may be times when the pastoral council best exercises its responsibility for pastoral planning by empowering a planning team that will take the lead in implementing the pastoral planning process on behalf of the council. The planning team reports its key outcomes to the council for its affirmation and ultimately for recommendation to the pastoral leader. After a thorough and prayerful discussion of the need for pastoral planning, the pastoral council should appoint a planning team. This should be a formal action of the council and should include clear references to the nature of pastoral planning. This book can be handy resource for that. It is important that both those appointed to the planning team and the wider parish community understand what pastoral planning is and what it is not. The following is a review of the advantages and disadvantages of appointing a planning team.

A. ADVANTAGES

The appointment of a separate planning team is a clear signal that pastoral planning is not business as usual. A separate structure with a new group of people sends strong signals to all involved that the parish and its leadership are open to new directions. Planning teams provide the opportunity to attract human resources needed by the parish but which ordinarily might not be available. The shorter time frame and clearer focus of the planning task contrasted to the more diffuse work of the pastoral council makes it easier for busy people, especially young professionals, to make the necessary time commitment. Establishing a planning team can also present the opportunity to include people who, for whatever reasons, do not find themselves on the pastoral council: youth, young adults, senior citizens, migrant workers, single mothers, the poor, the unemployed, and other groups often left on the margins.

Planning teams exist only for the active period of planning and so do not raise issues of structures and relationships and succession of membership and leadership. It has an agenda focused on the important concerns of the parish rather than trying to deal with all the diverse ministries of a typical contemporary parish. Without a status quo to worry about, a planning team finds it easier to be creative and "think outside the box."

B. DISADVANTAGES

There are some disadvantages to using a planning team. It is a new group, and thus time and energy must be devoted to recruiting membership, discerning leadership, and completing formation before the work of planning can begin. It is necessary to make the relationships between the planning team and other parish entities explicit. While this may be very helpful, it takes time and may unearth conflicts with constituencies that feel they have been left out of the process. Members of the planning team may not be well connected with the informal leadership of the parish because they might represent parishioners new to the leadership of the parish. Since the active planning is moved outside the pastoral council, where relationships with staff have typically attained some level of effectiveness, there can be especially touchy issues regarding the role of staff with a planning group.

Path Forward

Once parish leadership has made a decision on the organizational structure for planning, it should put together an initial plan for planning: a path forward, a default option on how to go about the process. A chart with a minimum of text is often the most effective way to present this path forward. This can be a simple flow chart showing the time and process relations between major tasks. Gantt charts showing key events, deadlines, and responsibilities help participants keep their bearings throughout the process and provide people with a simple and easy-to-understand overview of the whole process. A sample parish chart is shown below.

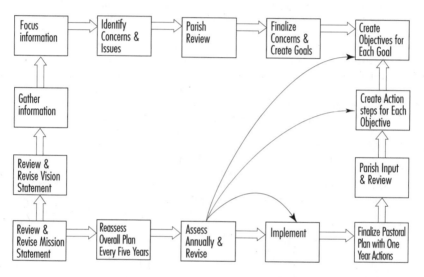

This initial plan should include a communication component so the entire parish understands the why and what of the process. This initial communication is the basis for communication throughout the process (see chapter 8 on communication), but it is essential that it be available in several different ways as the process begins. It can and should take many forms. Following is an example of such an initial communication that might be used as a letter from the pastoral leader to the members of the community, bulletin insert, or opening page on the parish web site for pastoral planning.

It has been several years since St. X Parish has reviewed its strategic plan. At several pastoral council discussions last year, it became clear that we needed to take a step back and look at where we are as a parish, where we want to go, and what we need to do to get there. Last May the Council recommended to me that we initiate a pastoral planning process for St. X Parish. I enthusiastically agreed, and we worked over the summer to prepare to begin that process this year.

The Council also recommended that we convene a special planning team to accomplish this important task. This will permit the Council to continue its important work in several ministry areas and to give quality attention to the recommendations coming from the planning effort. Every member of the parish community will have the opportunity to respond to recommendations by the planning team before they are presented to the parish pastoral council. Further, we will use our normal parish discernment and affirmation processes to consider each major component of the plan as well as the complete, final plan.

We are engaging in this process because we must be constantly assessing the signs of the times and their implications for what we do as individuals and as a parish. We understand pastoral planning to be the process of praying and thinking together about the actions of the Body of Christ in a specific time and place. We will review and possibly revise our mission statement and vision statement and will take into account five-year trend data about the parish and the larger community. We will share our conclusions with you at every step and will provide easy ways for you to provide us with your wisdom and input.

Ultimately, we will focus on three to five goals that we think will make system-wide differences in the way we respond to our call to be disciples of Jesus Christ. Our intent is not to have a plan that covers everything we do but to focus on a vital few that will make a resonating difference in our work.

The planning team is representative of the parish, and I want to thank those who have agreed to serve in this capacity, especially _____ and ___, who have agreed to serve as co-chairs. Attached to this you will find a list of the members, a simple flow chart and timeline, along with a brief description of the process we will follow. If you have any questions or concerns, please contact me, the chair or any member of the pastoral council, or the co-chairs of the planning team. Their e-mail addresses and phone numbers are below.

Finally I ask you to pray for this planning work. The planning team, the pastoral council, the parish staff, and major ministry groups have committed to saying together and reflecting on a wonderful prayer ascribed to Archbishop Oscar Romero. You will find that attached as well. Please pray for us, as we will for you. Together we will continue to build a strong, vibrant parish, a community of those called to discipleship in Jesus Christ.

Parish leadership should be mindful of two important points about implementation. First, an initial plan or path forward is essential for a team to successfully complete a new and challenging task. But in order for a team to be successful, it must make even an excellent plan its own by making some changes. This process of appropriating the process is absolutely essential to a vital and active team. The pastoral leader and co-chairs must be alert to this team development process and permit it to occur in a healthy way with a thorough discussion and open consensus. Leadership that obstructs that process or becomes defensive and protective will only slow the team development process and make an effective outcome less likely. Leadership must be mindful of the role of leadership in a community of disciples: to serve, not to be served.

Second, from initial conversations through to final affirmation, the process must proceed in a prayerful manner and must connect to everyone's experience of God working in his or her life. Leaders need to establish the expectation of faith sharing at every meeting from the very beginning of the process.

Parish Pastoral Planning Process

The generic process described in chapter 4 is the basis for the following description of the parish pastoral planning process. Only brief mention will be made of elements for which there is little or no adjustment needed at this level of planning. More time will be spent on those elements or concerns that are especially relevant to a parish.

MISSION STATEMENT

The assessment and revision or development of a mission statement will follow the process described in chapter 4. With appropriate and obvious changes in the sample forms, the process provides a default option for this part of the process. Town meetings, websites, focus groups, and individual conversations are used to obtain input. Chapter 8, on communication, contains details on these techniques.

VISION STATEMENT

A vision statement for the parish may not exist even though a mission statement does. The processes and forms in chapter 4 can be used with appropriate and obvious adjustments. To obtain quality input from the parish community, it may be necessary to explain what a vision statement is and how it functions in the pastoral planning cycle. Input and reaction processes will be the same as for the mission statement.

ASSESSING WHERE WE ARE / GATHERING INFORMATION

Having determined the mission and desired future state of the parish, the planning team needs to gather, focus, and make useful information relevant to the parish as the community of disciples. This information will focus on the operation and activities of the parish, the human conditions within the parish boundaries or other geographic area of focus, assessment of the key pastoral areas for the parish, relevant policy guidelines/constraints, and other information.

A. PARISH INFORMATION

Qualitative information about the key pastoral areas will be gathered in a subsequent process. This step looks at quantitative information about the parish and its activities. Of course, counting people or events does not give a complete picture of the vitality of a parish, but without the reality testing of these reports, planning teams can often fool themselves. We all want our parish to be healthy and vital, and this desire may make us overlook a gradual but persistent decline in the number of people attending Sunday Masses, for example. While such a fact does not fully describe the vitality of the parish, it is an important piece of information that can raise relevant, if uncomfortable, questions.

I. MASS ATTENDANCE REPORT

Many parishes count the number of attendees at Sunday Masses every week. (Sunday Masses include any Mass of anticipation on Saturday.) Most are in dioceses that require reports of attendance for an entire month, usually October. Unfortunately, these data are rarely transformed into useful information and then shared with parish members and leadership. The following form uses information for each Mass every weekend for the same month each year. Some parishes will have seasonal variations in attendance. This is often a factor for parishes located in summer or winter vacation areas or for those whose members relocate to warmer climates for winter months. While these may require special reports, the standard report, typically in October, will facilitate comparisons with other parishes.

**Sample Mass Attendance Information Form
and Worksheet** (Chart available at avemariapress.com)

Mass	First Weekend	Second Weekend	Third Weekend
One			
Two			
Three			
Four			
Total			
Total Capacity			
Capacity Used			
Church Capacity			

Sample Mass Attendance Information Form
and Worksheet (Continued)

Fourth Weekend	Total	Average	Capacity Used

This form assumes four weekend Masses and four weekends in the month. The seating capacity of the church is the actual seating capacity, not the maximum allowable by local fire codes, which usually includes some standing capacity. Whatever the capacity figure, it should be constant through the period of analysis.

Instructions for Completing Mass Analysis Form

1. Enter seating capacity.
2. Enter the attendance at each Mass in the appropriate cell for each weekend.
3. At the end of the month, calculate totals for each Mass (rows) and for each weekend (columns).
4. Then calculate the averages by dividing by the number of weekends (remember that some months have five weekends) and the number of Masses.
5. Calculate the capacity used for each Mass by dividing the average attendance per Mass by the seating capacity.
6. Calculate the total available capacity for each weekend by multiplying the capacity by the number of Masses.
7. Calculate the capacity used for each weekend by dividing total attendance by the total available capacity.
8. Convert all the results into percentages.

While this report provides useful information about the attendance at the different Masses on a typical weekend, it is a snapshot and does not disclose any trends. This same form for the previous five years provides that information. The following is a sample report generated from such a five-year history.

A Concise Guide to Pastoral Planning

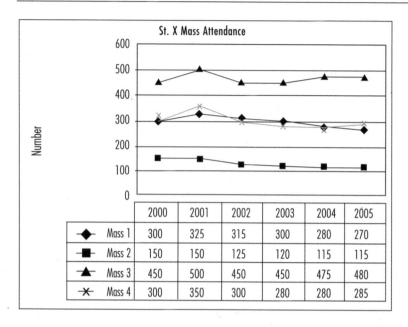

St. X Mass Attendance

		2000	2001	2002	2003	2004	2005
◆	Mass 1	300	325	315	300	280	270
■	Mass 2	150	150	125	120	115	115
▲	Mass 3	450	500	450	450	475	480
✳	Mass 4	300	350	300	280	280	285

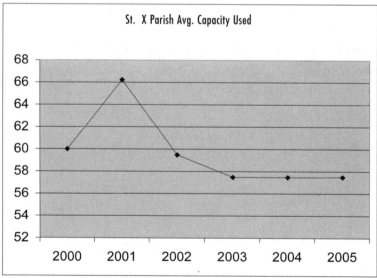

St. X Parish Avg. Capacity Used

The information displayed in this fashion helps the planning team ask good questions about the trends apparent in the information.

II. SACRAMENTAL REPORT

Each parish keeps careful records of the sacramental life of the parish. Over a five-year period, this information provides important insights into the dynamics of the parish. The following sample form shows a report and then a graphic presentation.

Sample Sacramental Parish Information Form						
	Year One	Year Two	Year Three	Year Four	Year Five	Total
Baptisms						
Confirmations						
Weddings						
Funerals						

It is easier to identify trends when this information is graphed. Setting this same information to a base index of 100 displays the rate of change of variables of different size in a comparable fashion. Chapter 7, on regional planning, will go into the detail of this technique.

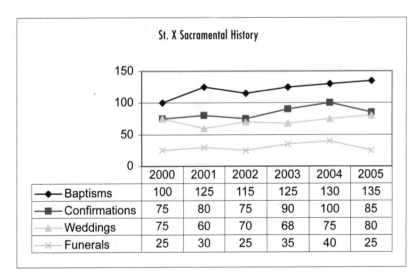

St. X Sacramental History

	2000	2001	2002	2003	2004	2005
Baptisms	100	125	115	125	130	135
Confirmations	75	80	75	90	100	85
Weddings	75	60	70	68	75	80
Funerals	25	30	25	35	40	25

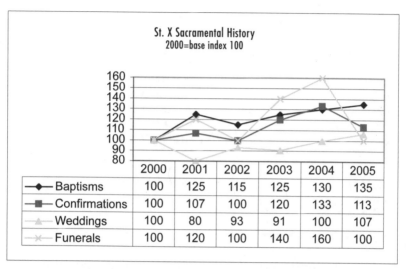

St. X Sacramental History
2000=base index 100

	2000	2001	2002	2003	2004	2005
Baptisms	100	125	115	125	130	135
Confirmations	100	107	100	120	133	113
Weddings	100	80	93	91	100	107
Funerals	100	120	100	140	160	100

III. PARTICIPANTS

Parishes have a great variety of programs: religious education for children, sacramental preparation, youth ministry, adult education, social ministries, liturgical functions, etc. A comprehensive list of ministries, including both those that support the faith community of the parish and those that announce the Reign of God in the external community, is an excellent starting point for this analysis. Often parishioners, even those very familiar with the parish, are surprised to see how many programs and ministries the parish supports. The following is an illustrative though not exhaustive list. Each planning team should work to develop its own list relevant to its parish.

Illustrative Parish Ministries	
Social Ministry	Sacramental Preparation
Stephen Ministry	Rite of Christian Initiation for Adults (RCIA)
School Partnerships	Parish Visitors
Religious Education	Health Care Ministry
Youth Ministry	Divorced/Separated
Young Adult Ministry	Refugee Resettlement
Men's Group	Rural Parish Support
Women's Group	Liturgical Ministries
Seniors	Catholic Elementary School
Adult Education	Catholic High School
Prison Ministry	
Food Cupboard	

The planning team gathers information on the number of people participating in and volunteering for each ministry over a five-year period. For example, there might be one hundred children participating in religious education and twenty adults volunteering as teachers. These statistics provide a comprehensive and detailed picture of the growth or decline of the parish in specific ministry areas. An important measure is the proportion of the parish members involved in these ministries. This can be estimated by dividing the number of participants in each ministry by the number of registered parishioners, the number of registered households, or the average number of weekend Mass attendees. In some cases, relevant subgroups provide better information: for example, the proportion of children in religious education to the total number of children in the parish. This statistic is not meant to be an absolutely precise measure of the percentage involved but rather a rough estimate that can be tracked over time. Relating participation to the number attending each weekend provides a measure that reflects both the scale of the parish and the overall level of involvement.

IV. PARISH DEMOGRAPHICS

The number of parishioners is the basic demographic measure for any parish. If one could know only one number about a parish, it would be its membership. There are different ways to measure size, as shown below.

Sample Demographic Parish Information Form (Chart available at avemariapress.com)						
	Year One	Year Two	Year Three	Year Four	Year Five	Total
Registered Households						
Registered Members						
Registered Within Year						
Formally Left Parish						
Number of Catholics Within Parish Boundaries						

Presented graphically, this information can be used to spot trends and changes. Other descriptors are also important and can be included albeit in a somewhat different format. Racial/ethnic and age profiles shown as bar charts can be very helpful. While these typically do not change dramatically over a short period, they present information that is often not apparent to the casual observer.

V. FINANCIAL

A review of the financial operations of a parish is an essential part of planning assessment. As pointed out earlier, a parish is not a corporation seeking to maximize profit. It is a community that exists for ministry. But just as St. Paul often pointed out to the churches he founded, there are real-world obligations to which we must attend. In contemporary language, we can say that the bottom line of a parish is not a financial but a pastoral one. At the same time, without reasonable financial health a parish may not be able to carry out the pastoral mission to which it is called. A balanced concern with finances is recognition of the reality of the Incarnation: a parish is a manifestation of the Spirit of God in a fully human organization.

While financial analysis can become quite complex, a fairly simple approach provides the key information needed for pastoral planning. As with other information, a five-year history provides the opportunity to identify changes and trends that might not be apparent with an annual analysis. The following is a sample financial analysis form.

Sample Financial Analysis Form (Chart available at avemariapress.com)							
	Year One	Year Two	Year Three	Year Four	Year Five	Total	Average
Regular Collections							
Other Income							
Total Income							
Pastoral Leader Staff Expense							
Other Staff Expense							
Program Expense							
Buildings and Grounds							
Other							
Total Expense							
Net Revenue							
Accumulated Net Revenue							

Regular collections include the weekly Sunday collections including envelopes, direct deposit, and plate cash. Special collections, unless for **current** parish operations or deficit reduction, should be included in "other income," along with bequests and special non-operating gifts. Larger parishes may have more sophisticated accounting systems that include unrestricted and restricted accounts. Such parishes can produce more complex reports. However, for the purposes of pastoral planning, simpler reports are often enough to answer questions about financial vitality.

Typically, a parish's major expense item is staff salaries and benefits. However, it is important to distinguish between those expenses associated with the pastor or pastoral leader and those with the other parish staff (both administrative and pastoral). It is important that the planning team gain an understanding both of the parish's ability to support pastoral leadership and staff and of the way that capacity might be changing through time. It is also important for the planning team to consider the extent to which the parish is paying appropriate salaries and benefits given the work demands of and educational preparation for pastoral roles. It needs to be particularly attentive to economic justice, both in terms of salary and service expected. There need to be appropriate arrangements for vacation, retreats, and professional development for parish staff.

Program expenses can be accumulated for all pastoral programs. A more detailed analysis may allocate both staff and program costs to specific programs or program categories, but aggregated analysis is usually sufficient for pastoral planning at this level. Building and grounds expenses should only reflect operating expense. Capital needs and expenditures will be included in the section following.

Net revenue is calculated by subtracting total expense from total revenue. An accumulated total net revenue figure will take into account annual variations and timing issues through a five-year period. Any of these data series can be presented in graph form, which will assist in identifying changes and trends. The intent at this point is not to arrive at any conclusions but rather to notice important items and trends for later inclusion in decision making.

One final piece of analysis will be helpful. Envelope users constitute the core of financial support for almost all parishes. It is important to track the number of envelope users as a proportion of total registered households and to track the total given by envelope users as a percentage of total income. Finally, the average annual contribution by envelope users is an excellent measure of the underlying financial health of a parish.

VI. BUILDINGS AND GROUNDS

In the Catholic Church, parishes traditionally have churches, which provide the location and environment for worship and celebration of Sunday Eucharist. In the United States, a church building has typically been expanded or additional facilities added to provide space for rectories, convents, gathering space, education, recreation, and parish life. Most parishes, in fact, have campuses composed of several buildings, parking lots, shrines, gardens, and set-back property. These physical assets must be tended to and maintained. Contemporary accounting standards require not-for-profit organizations to depreciate their physical assets and facilities to take account of this necessary maintenance. This was designed to reduce the use of deferred maintenance as a way of balancing stressed operating budgets. Deferred maintenance does not eliminate the need for maintenance and, in fact, tends to increase the cost of the maintenance when finally performed. Buildings may not have voices in the budget process, but when they must be fixed we hear them loud and clear!

An information sheet should be completed for each building and should include the major capital or maintenance items to be addressed over the next five or ten years. Particular emphasis should be placed on overdue maintenance items since these must be addressed with a higher priority. The total cost on an annual basis of the maintenance should be reflected in the reports. Any new structures contemplated or in planning should also be described. Total cost as well as annual operating costs should be included and funding sources for both indicated.

Sample Building Information Form (Chart available at avemariapress.com)	
Name	Date Constructed
Address	Square Feet
General Description	
Major Function	
General Condition	
Replacement Value	Market Value

Rate Building Systems with 5=excellent and 1=poor
    Roof
    Exterior
    Windows
    Heating/Cooling
    Plumbing
    Electrical
    Lighting
    Interior Wall Surfaces
    Floor
    Special Issues (Specify)
    Liturgical Space	

Annual Maintenance and Operating Cost	
Five-year Capital Improvement Needs (Items and Estimated Cost)	
Deferred Maintenance (Items and Estimated Cost)	

B. EXTERNAL COMMUNITY INFORMATION

The two sources of demographic information discussed in chapter 4 can be used for parish analysis. The Census website can be used to provide a wealth of information by zip codes and by census tracts. Typically parish boundaries do not follow zip code boundaries (which don't change) or census tracts (which do change with every census). Also, zip codes are not uniform in either geography or population, making comparison among them somewhat problematic. However, we are familiar with zip codes and have a good grasp of our own and neighboring zip codes. This makes them valuable in this level of analysis. Of course, as discussed in chapter 4, Ministry Area Profiles generated by Percept provide the most precise and complete analysis, especially tuned to pastoral planning. This information helps us spot changes in demographics that will alert us to ministry needs. It also invites us to compare and contrast parish and external community demographics to identify areas where the community of disciples no longer reflects the larger world of the parish. Relying on our own sense of change is usually not as reliable as viewing the data and information.

C. EVALUATING KEY AREAS OF PASTORAL CONCERN

Each planning team needs to focus on the five key pastoral areas or some schema that is more meaningful to the local situation. It may be that the diocesan church has a format for analysis of the pastoral life of a parish. In that case, that format should be used. Whatever is used, it is important that it be comprehensive so that all areas of parish life are considered. This analysis is more qualitative than quantitative. A team of people—composed of at least one member of the planning team, staff, and key lay ministry leaders knowledgeable of relevant ministries—review each pastoral area. They discuss the open-ended questions for each pastoral area. The discussion should be wide-ranging and open even if it does not address each question. The results of the discussion and review are written up. It is not necessary to arrive at a consensus; diverse—even opposed—opinions are helpful at this stage of the process. The following questions are illustrative but not exhaustive. As with other sections, it is important that the team appropriate the questions to ensure that the ones they are interested in are being asked.

Questions for Pastoral Area: Word

1. In what ways does the parish express the central role of scripture, especially the New Testament, in the life of the parish?
2. How do religious education, youth, young adult, and sacramental preparation ministries demonstrate the parish's constantly unfolding understanding of scripture, tradition, teaching of the Church, and the ongoing action of God as revelations of God's love and care for all reality?
3. What are the opportunities for and support of theological education for pastoral staff and parishioners?
4. In what ways does the parish respond to the call of Jesus Christ to discipleship through a radical commitment to stewardship? How does the parish identify and foster the vocations of members, especially those called to ordained ministry?

Questions for Pastoral Area: Worship

1. How do Eucharistic liturgies foster the full, active, and conscious participation envisioned by Vatican II?
2. How do sacramental celebrations strengthen the parish's response to the call to discipleship?
3. In what ways do Sunday Masses reflect a warm spirit of hospitality and openness to strangers in the midst of the assembly?
4. How do Sunday celebrations reflect a spirit of joy and life that seems to draw people to the parish?
5. How do liturgical ministers reflect the diversity of the parish, especially in terms of youth, young adults, seniors, ethnic minorities, sexual orientation, and those with disabilities? How does the liturgy itself reflect this diversity and inclusiveness?

Questions for Pastoral Area: Community

1. What are the ways in which the parish builds a sense of community among its members?
2. How are small groups used to create a sense of belonging, especially in very large parishes?
3. How does the parish welcome new members?
4. Do people feel there are insiders and outsiders? If yes, why? If no, why not?
5. What ministries focus on building up the community of faith?

Questions for Pastoral Area: Service
1. How does the parish express its mission in words and actions? 2. What ministries focus on announcing the Reign of God to the world, especially to those who have been discounted by the world? 3. Outside the parish membership, who would miss the parish if it no longer existed? Why? 4. In what ways have the outreach ministries of the parish changed in the past five years to reflect changes in the world?

Questions for Pastoral Area: Temporalities
1. Does the parish face any special challenges in maintaining viability over the next five years? If so, what are they, and how does the parish intend to deal with them? 2. In what ways does the parish express its relationship with the larger church: other parishes, other faith communities, and the diocese?

D. ASSESSING GUIDELINES AND CONSTRAINTS

A parish does not exist in a vacuum but is part of the larger Church. It also operates within a civil society with laws regulating corporate and individual behavior. While the team does not need to document all the policies and constraints within which it must operate, it is important to specify the ones most salient to the planning task.

These include:

1. Canon law
2. Policies and practices of the diocesan church
3. Explicit planning guidelines from the local bishop
4. Pastoral letters from the local bishop addressing relevant issues
5. The parish's own practice and values.

E. LOOKING AT OTHER INFORMATION: PARISHIONER SURVEYS

The generic process described in chapter 4 included the possibility of other information. For parishes this is often direct input of the attitudes, values, and desires of the members of the parish. Chapter 8, on communication, describes briefly the methods and issues involved in doing valid survey research. This information is very important to the planning process, especially information on the pastoral issues and concerns of the parishioners and their assessment of the effectiveness of current ministry programs. This information can often provide invaluable guidance to a planning team as it begins its work.

The above represents a tremendous amount of information. That is important to ensure a full reconsideration by the planning team rather than proceeding on its presuppositions about the parish and its issues. However, it presents an organizational challenge. Two principles can guide this work. First, the information collection in each of these areas does not need to be sequential; that is, work can be underway simultaneously in all these areas rather than completing the first before moving the second. Second, sub-teams composed of one or two members of the planning team and several other members drawn from relevant staff, lay ministry leaders, and parishioners with special expertise in an area or in data collection and summation techniques are best able to do this work. Sub-team members from the planning team serve as liaison to the planning team. This can also be very effective in overall engagement of the parish community, thus spreading information about the process through informal channels of communication as well as formal.

STEPS FOUR THROUGH ELEVEN

From this point on, the parish pastoral planning process follows the generic process described in chapter 4. Each of the following steps is described in that chapter and, with appropriate adaptations, can be used in the parish process.

- Focus Information
- Identification of Concerns, Issues, and Ideals
- Engagement of the Parish Community
- Revision and Finalization of Mission, Vision, Issues/Opportunities
- Development of Goals
- Development of Objectives
- Development of Action Steps
- Engagement of the Parish Community
- Affirmation
- Implementation and Assessment

IMPORTANT RELATIONSHIPS

Within every planning level there are important relationships with individuals and groups. The parish pastoral planning process needs to be clear about these relationships.

A. PASTOR OR PASTORAL LEADER

Every parish has a pastor or someone appointed by the bishop to serve as pastoral leader. The pastor represents the authority and pastoral care of the bishop for a specific parish. In dioceses where there are not enough priests to appoint a priest as pastor for every parish, the bishop may appoint a lay person or a deacon or a team of people to fulfill that function. This is done in light of canon 517§2 that permits such appointments if there is a shortage of priests. Such a pastoral leader also embodies the bishop for that particular community. In addition, a pastor or pastoral leader is accountable to the bishop for the vitality and vibrancy of the parish. The five areas of pastoral concern (or some other schema promulgated by the bishop in line with canon law) provide the focus for this accountability. There may also be local diocesan legislation that lays out other requirements for parishes, for example, the presence of a pastoral council or the role of Catholic schools in the life of a parish.

The pastor may also be empowered by the people of the parish as their leader, but his formal authority derives from the bishop. In a well functioning parish, there is no conflict between the informal authority of the pastor and the formal authority derived from the structure of the Church. As such, the pastor is the decision maker for all formal actions of the parish. The pastoral planning process and structure must respect this position of the pastor. As noted at the beginning of this chapter, it is essential that the pastoral planning begin with the pastor or pastoral leader. While the pastoral council may affirm the pastoral plan, it does so technically as a consultative body to the pastor. No pastor can accept decisions that seriously impact the parish without hearing the voice of the parishioners, both directly and through a pastoral council. If this is clearly understood at the beginning and throughout the process of planning, many problems can be eliminated.

Pastors also need to understand the effective relationship between his authority and the rights and responsibilities of the members of the parish. Unilateral decisions, no matter whether they are right or wrong, will erode the vitality of the parish community. If a pastoral leader finds it necessary to oppose some elements of a plan, he or she should be clear about this as early as possible in the process, be open to changing his or her position as the process unfolds, and make clear the grounds for opposition. At the same time, the parish and its leadership need to understand and respect the responsibilities and authority of the pastor. In short, a collaborative working relationship with good communication is the key to living with this often-ambiguous situation.

B. FINANCE COUNCIL

Every parish has a finance council with whom the pastor must consult about significant financial decisions and issues. The review and approval of the annual operating and capital improvement budget of the parish must involve the finance council. The pastoral council and/or planning team must also respect this role of the finance council. It is essential that some members of the finance council be members of the pastoral council and/or planning team. This ensures that the finance council is well informed about the development of the pastoral plan and especially about the financial implications of plans. It is always problematic if the plan is presented to the finance council only at the very end of the process. The finance council then feels it is in an impossible situation to bring financial reality to an already completed plan. At the same time, the finance council needs to understand its role and not begin to make decisions about pastoral priorities and ministries solely on financial grounds.

C. STAFF

In many parishes, the pastoral and administrative staff is quite developed and plays a central role in the pastoral life of the parish. Thus it is essential that staff be represented on the planning team and perhaps on the pastoral council. One effective model is to make sure that the staff attends pastoral council meetings to provide its experience and wisdom for the council's deliberations. It is in the development of goals, and especially of objectives and action steps, that the staff must play a proactive role. In some parishes lay ministry leaders play a similar role and should also be included.

D. PASTORAL COUNCIL

When the pastoral council empowers a planning team to do the direct planning work, it is essential that it be kept informed of the process and especially of issues that may lead to fundamental changes in the life of the parish. The planning team should include members of the pastoral council whose role is to keep the pastoral council informed of progress of the plan. The planning team leadership should provide regular briefings for the council, and the council should be invited to react in-depth at each stage of the process.

Conclusion

In this chapter we have discussed the application of the generic pastoral planning process to parish pastoral planning. We reviewed the initial questions of organization: using the pastoral council or a planning team. We rather thoroughly reviewed the types of information used in the process, along with forms for data collection and analysis and sample graphs. The result will be a pastoral plan that provides the major emphases for a parish over a five-year period. These are the key changes that will move the parish toward its envisioned future. Next we turn to diocesan pastoral planning.

Study Questions

1. What do you think makes the most sense in our situation: pastoral council or planning team? What are your reasons for your answer?
2. What would you add to the letter introducing pastoral planning to the faith community?
3. What do you think are the most important measurements of vitality for your parish or faith community? What would you add or subtract from those in this chapter?
4. How would you change the questions in the key pastoral areas assessment? Would you add or subtract areas?
5. The relationship with the pastoral leader (pastor or pastoral administrator) is very important. Are you clear about the relationship between him or her and the pastoral council, finance council, and the bishop? What questions do you have?

CHAPTER 6

Implementation at the Diocesan Level

In this chapter we will describe the ways in which we can apply the generic pastoral planning process to a diocesan church. With appropriate adjustments for scale, we can easily apply much of what has been presented in chapter 4 on the generic process and in chapter 5 on the parish process to the diocesan church. However, dioceses face some planning issues and concerns not faced by either individual parishes (chapter 5) or regional groupings of parishes (chapter 7.) We will discuss these special topics after a review of the pastoral planning process itself.

We will begin with a discussion of the organizational questions as we did with parishes. We will then discuss the importance of a clear beginning as well as the necessary focus for diocesan planning. Next, we will review the special concerns raised by the greater diversity found in dioceses as opposed to parishes and the relationships to significant positions and groups. After a review of the application of the generic process to dioceses, we will conclude with a discussion of three special topics: strategic planning, special planning projects, and staffing for planning.

Organizational Issues

Just as individual parishes do, dioceses face the question of how to best organize for pastoral planning. Although most do, not every diocese has a diocesan pastoral council (DPC), a group broadly representative of the diocese that discovers and ponders pastoral issues and develops creative and effective responses to them. Since this is the core work of pastoral planning, it would seem natural that a DPC would carry out pastoral planning. If this is not possible or advisable, then the DPC acting with the diocesan bishop should empower a planning team that will do the direct work of pastoral planning and make its recommendations to the DPC, which, in turn, will advise the bishop. As with the pastor or pastoral leader of a parish, it is the bishop who makes the final decision to accept and implement the pastoral plan.

The advantages and disadvantages of using an existing DPC or of creating a planning team are essentially the same as those described for the parish context. In brief, using the DPC will reduce the number of entities involved, make use of existing working relationships, enhance and clarify the role of the DPC, and provide it with an ongoing role of serving as a point of accountability for implementation. The disadvantages accrue from its existing relationships and operational procedures. It may well be difficult for an existing DPC to sense new pastoral issues and to create novel and dramatically different responses. The inertia of doing business as usual may prove simply too strong to admit of any fundamental change.

A specially appointed planning team would make clear that planning is not business as usual. It also has the advantage of permitting the recruitment of people who might not find themselves as members of a DPC. Since a DPC is by its nature representative, its membership may not always include people with the skills, information, and background needed for effective pastoral planning. The time-limited nature and clear focus of the planning process makes service on a planning team attractive to people who might otherwise not be able to make the kind of long-term, ongoing commitment required by a DPC. However, the formation of a planning team takes time and resources, may delay the beginning of pastoral planning, requires formation of planning team members, and may create confusion about the relationship with the DPC, diocesan finance council, priests' council, and other standing diocesan entities and consultative bodies. Use of a planning team also runs the risk of creating the perception that outsiders, in the sense of those outside the normal consultative processes, are making the decisions.

Weighing the advantages and disadvantages of either approach and diagnosing the planning issues faced by the diocese, the bishop will decide which approach to take. The methodology described in the parish process about the formation of a special team can be easily applied in a diocesan setting.

The bishop may decide that it is best to convene a diocesan synod for the purpose of pastoral planning. The role, nature, membership, and methodology of a diocesan synod are described in canons 460–468. It is not within the scope of this work to go into a detailed consideration of synods. However, even dioceses that have convened synods have found that an ongoing process of pastoral planning is better entrusted to a DPC or a planning team.

Path Forward

The first step in beginning pastoral planning is to communicate to all audiences the initiation of the process, the reasons for planning, and the process to be used. This is especially true at the diocesan level because of the complexity and size of the effort. It is not unusual that such an effort involves hundreds of thousands of members, hundreds of parishes and priests, thousands of lay ecclesial ministers, hundreds of diocesan employees, and the external community. Trying to keep one's bearings and to keep even simple relationships clear can be challenging. It is essential that the process begin with a clear statement of purpose that is referenced often throughout the process.

This foundational communication comes from the bishop—the pastor of the diocese—who is committed to pastoral planning as described in this book. A planning process that begins with the priests' council or the DPC but does not engage the appropriate time, support, and attention from the bishop will surely fail to reach its potential for change even if it is finally completed. The ordinary method for such communication is a pastoral letter from the bishop to all parishes and faith communities in the diocese. The letter from the pastoral leader of a parish with appropriate changes can serve as a model for this episcopal communication. Just as in the parish process, the path forward for a diocesan pastoral planning effort should include charts to provide an overview and more holistic description of the process. The charts included in chapter 5, with appropriate modifications, can be used to communicate the essentials of a diocesan process.

Focus

Focus is another issue that confronts diocesan planning. What is the focus of the planning? Does the bishop intend that the process will identify priority change goals for implementation by parishes and faith communities, by the diocesan ministries, or both? If the focus is to be on the changes necessary within parishes and other faith communities, then it is important to include planning team members from that constituency, in all its diversity. The specter of a central group, often isolated from the day-to-day reality of parishes, planning for what parishes need to do is often enough to sentence even a well-planned process to an inconclusive and painfully slow demise. If the focus is on diocesan ministries and the actions of the diocesan church, then it is important that this be clearly communicated and that appropriate diocesan ministries be involved. It is often the case that planning focuses on both.

The diocesan church creates a supportive context within which parishes and faith communities will live out their pastoral calls. It is tempting to think of these two as sequentially and hierarchically ordered so that there is a comprehensive plan from diocesan to parish level with each entity pursuing common and detailed objectives and goals. This is where there is a clear danger that secular corporate assumptions about structure and relationships may infect the planning process. It is tantalizingly easy to view the Church as composed of hierarchically ordered levels in which the higher level sets key policy, specifies strategic actions, sets standards for evaluation, and oversees lower levels for compliance. In this view the Vatican possesses perfect or near-perfect understanding, which it communicates to dioceses, which in turn communicate to parishes. Information and oversight flow down; compliance moves up. While there are aspects of such a system in the Church, they are for administrative efficiency. They do not reflect the essence of the Church as a communion of disciples.

At this point it is important to remind ourselves that we are about *pastoral* planning: the process of praying and thinking together about the actions of the Body of Christ in a specific time and place. This is essentially a spiritual process in which the Spirit of God is the actor. The heart of the matter is that the Church is the communion of the disciples of Jesus Christ, animated by the Spirit. The spirit moves this communion of communions in ways that do not necessarily follow bureaucratic organizational structures.

The reality is that the Church is composed of overlapping levels wherein Pope, bishops, and pastors have full and immediate authority in their spheres of activity. Only a collegial rather than an authoritarian approach will work in such a setting. Further, the simple imposition of authority will work against the core understanding of the Church as the Body of Christ, a communion of disciples.

It would be foolish to think that we can so completely understand the Spirit that we can capture in a comprehensive plan everything to which we are being led. It is important that the Spirit have room to operate within our dioceses and parishes. This room to operate may often appear to us to be those who think differently and behave differently. These are the people who are often our prophets, who call us back to a more faithful commitment to the call of our shared discipleship.

Diversity

Diocesan pastoral planning faces the issue of diversity to a greater extent than does parish pastoral planning. Parishes, even diverse ones, are homogenous when compared to the diocesan church. This is most evident when we try to describe the parishes of a diocese. We are tempted to use averages, but they can often hide more information than they uncover. A diocese that includes urban, suburban, exurban, small town/village, and rural parishes will find that an overall average will either not provide valid information about any type of parish or may be skewed toward the parishes that include the most people. Typically most people are members of suburban parishes that tend to be newer, larger, and wealthier than other types of parishes. Using overall averages to set or imply standards for all parishes will often create injustice rather than foster quality. In addition, at the diocesan level there are often specialized ministries that are not erected as parishes yet play an important role in the pastoral life of the diocese. These include campus ministries, prison ministries, health ministries, migrant ministries, and ministries focused on special populations, such as the deaf or hearing-impaired, the homebound, or people with special needs. Measures of sacramental life, for example, need to take these diverse faith communities into account. More important, however, any norms adopted for these communities must be based on their unique experience rather than on generalizations.

Ownership of the Process

Diocesan leadership, as parish leadership, needs to be mindful of the need for the planning team to appropriate the initial process described in the path forward provided by the bishop. This requires some period of conflict and disagreement about the process and a healthy way to make changes that reflect the ideas and commitment of the planning team. While this rarely results in substantial changes to the process, it is essential to the development of the team. It requires the bishop and the internal leadership of the planning team to understand this dynamic and to make the concessions necessary to allow the team to go through this essential stage of group development.

Prayer

From the very beginning, the diocesan pastoral planning process needs to be a prayerful one. This means more than the recitation of prayers at the beginning of the meeting. Faith sharing must be the foundation for pastoral planning, especially at the diocesan level. While people may have experienced faith sharing in small groups in their parish, it is unfortunately rare that they have experienced it in large meeting formats at the diocesan level. There is a tendency to see faith sharing as something that church people do in small groups rather than as something each of us does in all the settings of our lives. Often DPC and planning teams are composed of people who have come to these roles through their prominence in the larger community rather than through service in parishes. They can too often have a desire to get down to business and "get the prayers out of the way" so the real work can begin. It is essential that this attitude be changed at the very beginning of the process so the membership is softened to the action of the Spirit in their lives and thus in the work of planning. Even though diocesan planning teams or DPCs may have quite large memberships, it is possible to do fruitful faith sharing.

Diocesan Pastoral Planning Process

The diocesan pastoral planning process is based on the generic process described in chapter 4. A review of that chapter will provide the reader with the basics of the process and the interrelationships among the various elements. The flow begins with mission, vision, and then the gathering of information so that important issues and concerns can be identified. These then form the basis for major goals, for which objectives and then action steps are identified.

Implementation and assessment of results and processes are annual and ongoing, leading to a complete review every five years.

The larger scale of a diocese contrasted with a parish gives rise to issues of complexity, which are most apparent in communications and in gathering community input. The end result is that communications and information-gathering require more time to ensure that diverse constituencies are included and listened to. A diocese may already have a consultative structure in place that provides the bishop the opportunity to listen carefully to the voices of the faithful, including clergy and lay ecclesial ministers in his diocese. If such structures exist, they should be used to gather information from members of the diocese and to communicate information about the planning process to them. There is no necessity for creating additional structures if none are needed.

If such structures do not exist, or if they exist but do not take into account the geographic and cultural diversity of the diocese, new or revised structures should be considered. However, it is possible to use focus groups (as described in chapter 8, on communication), especially if convened regionally at various times and places throughout the diocese. These can provide valuable information as the planning process begins and can provide input and reaction at the consultation points throughout the process. Because of the scale and complexity, it is important that the results of the focus groups be written as public documents available to anyone who wants to review them. This is most easily accomplished on a diocesan pastoral planning website.

Diocesan websites are an especially important resource in supporting pastoral planning. Not only do they provide a mechanism for keeping members informed, they also provide a way for members to send input directly into the planning process. Sites can provide access to relevant diocesan documents and reports so that those interested can view and make hard copies if it seems appropriate. The following is an example of the site map of a diocesan pastoral planning website.

- Diocesan Pastoral Planning
  - History
  - Current Process
  - Planning Team
  - Timeline
  - Pastoral Letter
  - Reaction Drafts with Input Forms
  - Summaries of Reaction
- Mission
- Vision
- Goals
- Objectives
- Action Steps
- Resources
  - Diocesan Policies
  - Prayers and Faith Sharing
  - Other Diocesan Websites
- Parish Pastoral Planning
- Regional Pastoral Planning
- Diocesan Pastoral Council
- FAQs
- Contact Us
- Staff

Diocesan pastoral planning must always remain conscious of the diversity of the diocese in terms of geography, culture, ecclesiology, and spirituality. These differences are important not only to a realistic view of the diocesan church but also to the ongoing health and vitality of that church. Since pastoral planning at this level often is done by a few people, it is all too easy for them to assume that all members exhibit their culture, ecclesiology, or spirituality, and thus make inappropriate choices that are irrelevant to many. This underscores the importance of collecting information reflecting that diversity.

MISSION STATEMENT

The process to review, revise, and/or write a completely new mission statement is essentially the same as the generic process implemented at the parish level. The use of forms and the structured discussion at meetings of the planning team will be very similar. The focus must be on the entire diocese and this can often be challenging since many dioceses are very diverse. The writing of a mission statement for a diocese is more difficult than writing one for a parish because of the many and often competing voices to be heard and expressed. The forms presented in chapter 4 can be effectively used by people to prepare for focus groups that will deal with a review of a mission statement. While the parish process is based on a few people who are knowledgeable about the parish and its issues, a small group will find it very difficult to take that same perspective for the diocese. Each of us experiences church first and fundamentally in our parish or primary faith community. For most of us, we never experience the "diocesan church," and so find it difficult to achieve a view of the whole. As a result we need to rely on the perspectives of others and thus need to implement a process that involves and listens to them from the very beginning. Regional focus groups at the very beginning of the process are important ways to achieve this input, as well as an easy-to-use, interactive pastoral planning website.

VISION STATEMENT

A diocesan vision statement can be developed in the same fashion as a parish vision statement, with the adjustments required for diversity and change in scale. A vision is the view of where the diocese sees itself at some point in the future, usually a ten-year horizon, if the mission statement were being more completely achieved. It reveals the gap required for planning. We are here; we want to get to that future state described in the vision. What do we need to do to begin to move toward that future?

ASSESSING WHERE WE ARE / GATHERING INFORMATION

The same type of information collected for parishes forms the basis for information about the diocese. All of the parish information can be summed up to provide a picture of the diocese. This includes Mass attendance, sacramental information, participants, demographics, and parish financial information. This data can all be summed and presented as an overall picture of the diocese. Again, while snapshots are helpful and accurate, five-year histories provide the opportunity to spot trends and changes.

Given the large scale of a diocese, however, it is important to manipulate these data to provide more useful information. Averages and means are one way to describe the central tendencies of a large amount of data. While accurate, these can often hide information. It is important to look at relevant subgroups along with overall summary data to gain an understanding of the underlying dynamics of any large group of data. The following is an example of a diocesan report that shows both overall summary data and subgroup analysis. Clearly providing more detailed information helps get a clearer picture of the underlying reality.

The following is an example of a simple report that can provide relevant information over a five-year period. In the samples shown here, total baptisms have been increasing, but the experience of parishes varies in important ways by type of parish.

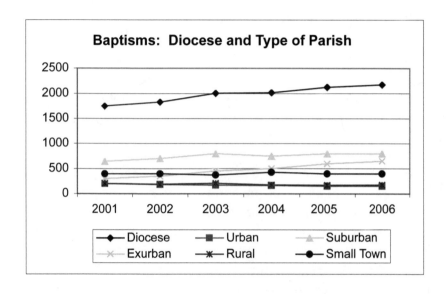

Baptisms: Diocese and Type of Parish

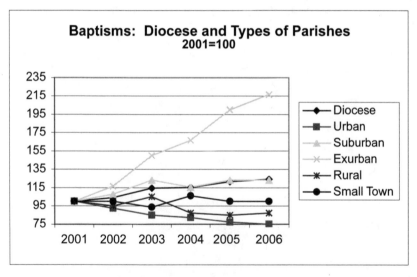

Baptisms: Diocese and Types of Parishes
2001=100

An important aspect of the financial picture of a diocese is the financial health of individual parishes. This can be measured by summing and subgroup analysis. However, there are additional financial issues that must be included to provide a full and complete picture of the financial state of the diocese, especially the operation of its central administration. Just as parish planners will benefit from reports that show the relative amounts of resources going into pastoral and administrative programs, the same is true for those doing diocesan planning. While the development of the information from the basic financial data is often far from simple, the reports themselves are typically fairly straightforward. A pie or bar chart is usually the best way to show the relative amount of resources allocated to specific areas. This provides an opportunity to see the relative importance of demands for resources in pastoral and administrative areas. As with all the reports and charts suggested in this work, these charts will gain in interpretive significance when the time dimension is added. This permits planners to see changes over time, not only of the absolute amounts provided but also of changes in the relative shares or demands.

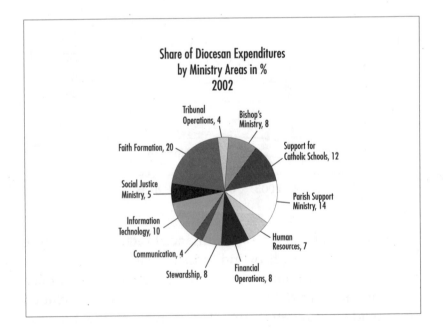

Share of Diocesan Expenditures by Ministry Areas in % 2002

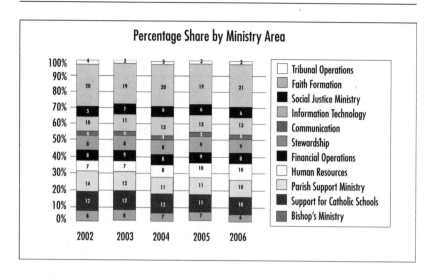

Percentage Share by Ministry Area

The same analysis can be performed for diocesan revenue showing the major sources of revenue, the revenue per relevant unit (contributions per known diocesans), and the share of total revenue provided by each sector. Adding a time variable of change over a five-year or even longer period will add to the information provided by these data. Sample reports are shown below.

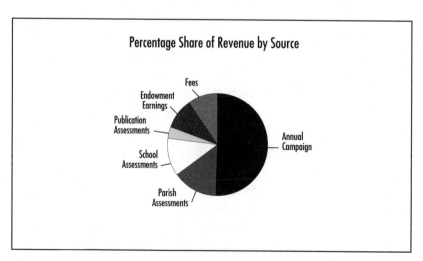

Percentage Share of Revenue by Source

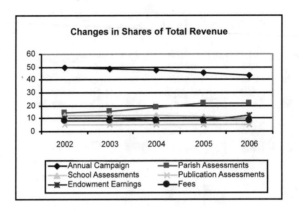

Changes in Shares of Total Revenue

Legend:
- Annual Campaign
- Parish Assessments
- School Assessments
- Publication Assessments
- Endowment Earnings
- Fees

One of the most challenging aspects of diocesan planning is the difficulty of making comparative judgments of financial and other information across different dioceses. While almost all dioceses make some kind of public report of revenue and expenses, the formats, especially when aggregated in ministry or administrative areas, are rarely similar enough to provide accurate comparisons. Often diocesan chief financial officers have good working relationships with their peers in other dioceses in their geographic area and are able to provide some comparable information. However, this level of detail is often not public information, which reduces its usefulness in the kind of planning process described in this book. While it may be difficult to provide comparable information across dioceses, it is possible and essential that diocesan financial and ministry information be categorized in a manner similar to that used for parish and other faith communities. While the language used in the parishes within even a single diocese is not always uniform, those doing parish and those doing diocesan planning within the same diocese should be able to look at the correspondence (or lack of it) between parish allocations and diocesan ones.

With regard to external community demographics, the summing of parish data will be helpful to the extent that the diocese is relatively homogeneous. To the extent that it is not, the averages used in the total information may not provide the best profile of the demographic changes in the diocese. A Ministry Area Profile (MAP) from Percept for the entire diocese, nonetheless, does provide very useful information. It becomes more useful to the extent that it can be performed on smaller geographic units of the diocese. This will be reviewed in the next chapter on regional planning. The U.S. Census Bureau is an important source of basic demographic information, especially for change in population and in the major descriptors of population. The Bureau performs annual updates of this information, and very readable summaries are typically available in the secular press. If special studies are needed, nearly every diocese contains a university or independent research organization that can provide specialized analysis. For national and regional changes and demographics, a regular review of *USA Today* and National Public Radio programming is very helpful.

A review of the five key pastoral areas is just as important for the diocesan church as it is for individual parishes. The questions used in the parish process, with appropriate adaptations, can be used for diocesan pastoral planning. In fact, it is essential that the same questions be used rather than create the perception that pastoral evaluation is something only done at the parish and not the diocesan level. While it is true that the diocesan church and its central staff have different types of responsibilities to the community of disciples, there should be a fundamental alignment between the two. It may be helpful and important to add additional questions for the diocesan review in light of this different role and emphasis, but these should be additions, not substitutions. The procedure for collecting this assessment is essentially the same as in the parish process. It is even more important that those who are familiar with the areas under consideration have the opportunity to provide input.

Because of the number and diversity of members of a typical diocese, surveys of attitudes, knowledge, and expectations can be very useful. People who are familiar with survey construction, administration, and analysis should conduct these assessments.

STEPS FOUR THROUGH ELEVEN

From this point on the diocesan pastoral planning process follows the generic process described in chapter 4. Each of the following steps is described in that chapter and with appropriate adaptations can be used in the diocesan process.

- Focus Information
- Identification of Concerns, Issues, and Ideals
- Engagement of the Diocesan Community
- Revision and Finalization of Mission, Vision, Issues/Opportunities
- Development of Goals
- Development of Objectives
- Development of Action Steps
- Engagement of the Diocesan Community
- Affirmation
- Implementation and Assessment

The result of this process is a five-year plan that addresses the major issues and change opportunities that the diocese will move definitively toward in order to more fully accomplish its mission. The plan will have taken into account the present reality of the diocese by going through a voluminous amount of information and sifting it down to the most important and salient issues. The whole process will have been used to educate, form, and involve members of the diocese in the planning process so that the resulting priorities represent the thinking of the entire diocese, not just a few chosen people.

The plan will include goals that will move the diocese towards this future. It will also have more detailed implementation plans, including action steps and a budget for the first of the five years. Toward the end of the first year of implementation, an assessment of it and a review of goals and objectives will generate a second-year plan. Pastoral planning, thus, becomes an ongoing process for the diocese.

Special Relationships

Within every diocese there are positions and groups with whom the planning team must have an effective working relationship. While the details of this process and structure will vary from diocese to diocese, these relationship issues must be understood and addressed.

A. DIOCESAN BISHOP

The diocesan bishop holds a special place in the human organization we call church. For those who have not been directly involved with the Church at the diocesan level, it is a tempting misunderstanding to see the bishop as the chief executive officer of this organization. While he is the CEO, he is much more and is called to exercise his leadership responsibility in a manner consistent with the call to discipleship to which we all, including the bishop, are called. There are many ways of understanding the role of bishop in the Roman Catholic tradition, and that role has changed in response to the needs and challenges of each age. However, the central role of the bishop is to ensure that the local (diocesan) Church is a vibrant expression of the Holy Spirit, who gathers the disciples of Jesus Christ together in a communion which is one, holy, catholic, and apostolic.

A bishop is called to ensure the ongoing unity of the Church to which he has been called. This is not a sterile uniformity but rather a unity that seeks what is in common while encouraging the vibrancy of difference in what is not central. A bishop is always concerned about the holiness of the church gathered about him. This is holiness not based on simply following the rules and behaving ethically, but is based on a real relationship between each member and the Lord Jesus Christ, who then calls us all into a community of faith so that we become God's people.

A bishop focuses on the catholicity of the Church in the sense that it is a communion of believers that is meant for all humans and is open to all. The only criterion for membership is a declared belief in the Creed and a life that reflects an honest attempt to follow the way of life of Jesus Christ. The bishop is always alert to any attempts to restrict membership on any other basis and to always teach about the Reign of God that is announced to all and for all. Finally, a bishop is called to maintain faithfulness to the message of Jesus Christ as we received it through the Apostles—those who were in direct human relationship with Jesus—who received the message first-hand, and whom Jesus commissioned to spread the message to the entire world. Of course, the message of Jesus was handed down within a specific cultural context and it must be announced and lived today within specific cultural contexts. Both the original context and all subsequent ones have impacted the message, not in essentials but in the human expressions of those essentials. Bishops are the ones that the Church looks to in the first place to be alert to those changes and to make those difficult judgments about what is of the essence and what is meant to change—indeed, what must change.

Bishops carry out their tasks in three ways. They teach. They celebrate sacraments. They provide servant leadership to the social organization we call church. To say the least, this is not an easy job, let alone an easy vocation. The best bishops draw the members of the diocese, both ordained and non-ordained, into an ongoing partnership on behalf of the local church.

Just as in the parish setting the pastor is the decision maker, so too in the diocesan setting the bishop is the decision maker. Canon law provides for consultation with knowledgeable members of the diocese and with those affected by certain decisions. However, a bishop who understands how modern organizations function best and who has been formed by the notions of leadership promoted by Jesus easily and freely shares his power and authority. He does this in ways that never diminish his ultimate responsibility to the larger church, to the members of his diocese, and to God for the oneness, holiness, catholicity, and apostolicity of the local church. A planning team and/or a diocesan pastoral council must always respect this role and its implications and never confuse this role with that of leadership roles in other organizations with which they may be more familiar.

For their part, bishops need to understand the dynamics of working with highly educated and empowered lay people typical of Catholics in twenty-first century United States and Canada. There are points in the planning process when the planning team may recommend, perhaps even strongly, a position which is not acceptable to the bishop as he reflects on his responsibilities for the local church. This is a situation that should be clearly understood by all involved. The best way to handle these divergences when they arise is to have the bishop provide rather complete feedback to the planning team and through them to the entire diocese about which of the recommendations he accepts and will implement and which ones he will not. In the latter case it is essential that he explain why the recommendation is not being followed or why it is being modified. In a well-formed planning team, a response that takes clear responsibility and lays out the reasons for action will strengthen the local church rather than disrupt it. Explicit and implicit explanations that resolve, "That's the way I am going to do it" do not build up the communion of disciples.

B. DIOCESAN FINANCE COUNCIL

By canon law (c. 492), every diocese is required to have a finance council that prepares an annual budget for the diocese and reviews the annual report of revenues and expenditures (c. 493). The bishop is required to consult with the diocesan finance council concerning important acts of administration and needs their consent for extraordinary acts as defined by national conferences of bishops (c. 1277).

Pastoral planning must respect the work of the finance council and should have explicit processes in place to keep the finance council informed about their work and the likely directions that might have important implications for the work of the finance council.

C. PRIESTS' COUNCIL

Also by canon law each diocese must have a presbyteral or priests' council. The function of the council is to aid the bishop in the governance of the diocese. It represents the priests of the diocese and is "like a senate of the bishop" (c495§1). Pastoral planning must respect the work of the priests' council and should have explicit processes in place to keep the council informed about the process and the likely directions that might have important implications for its work. Unlike the finance council, it is likely that the priests' council has been deeply involved in the decision to do pastoral planning. As well it is likely that some or perhaps several of the priests' council members have served as members of the planning team or the diocesan pastoral council. The priests' council reflects the thinking of the priests of the diocese and their essential role as pastors of the communion of disciples. It is not unusual for the priests' council to see the need for some type of pastoral planning before the bishop is willing to act on that recommendation. These men are pastors, dealing with the direct, day-to-day implications of trying to lead the People of God in today's culture. More than anyone else, they know of the necessity for making careful choices.

D. DIOCESAN STAFF

Diocesan staff is comprised of the diocesan curia, a group of professional administrators, and ministers who assist the bishop in carrying out his responsibility for the church. Their authority in most cases is a delegated authority from the bishop for specific ministries and tasks. They relate to parish pastoral leaders, parish staff, and lay ministry leaders as resources provided by the bishop for the growth in vitality of parishes and faith communities. This is often a nuanced role that they need to walk between facilitating and assisting on the one hand and overseeing on the other.

Since the planning process, as it moves toward the development of goals, objectives, and action steps is considering the work that may well have to be done by diocesan staff, it is imperative that they have a strong role in the development of these aspects of the plans. This is especially true when implementation requires restructuring of staff and offices and the reallocation of resources.

E. DIOCESAN PASTORAL COUNCIL

If a planning team is used for planning, its recommendations move to the DPC for consideration, modification, affirmation, and recommendation to the bishop. Since the planning team would have been created by the DPC, and since some members of the DPC would have been serving on the planning team, there should be few surprises in terms of recommendations for budget. Nonetheless, just because there is the potential for communication does not mean that communication actually takes place. Each planning team should at least name a representative to the DPC whose role is to keep the DPC informed about the work of planning.

Three Special Issues

There are three issues that are particularly relevant to diocesan pastoral planning: strategic planning, special planning projects, and staffing for planning. We will look at each of these as we close this chapter.

STRATEGIC PLANNING

Very often members of consultative groups prominent in the corporate world will press for the diocese and the bishop to engage in strategic planning as though that were something different from the pastoral planning process described above. In the corporate world, either profit or non-profit, strategic planning is a comprehensive planning process that seeks to maximize market share and net revenue through a careful allocation of resources and through process improvements. It is driven by scarcity of external resources and an organization's ability to identify, cultivate, and import external resources to support its production or service processes. It implies customers who choose to buy, donate, or invest limited resources and who have many options from which to choose. Such planning has demonstrated its usefulness in secular organizations.

While there are many terms and functions that seem similar in strategic planning and pastoral planning, they are in essence two different processes, neither of which can be substituted for the other. As a generic term, strategic planning might include pastoral planning as strategic planning for a community of disciples of Jesus Christ. However, even the language helps us understand the difference. We can easily appreciate the call for strategic planning if we primarily think of and refer to the church as a corporation, albeit with a religious goal and highly decentralized operations. If we think of the church primarily as a communion of those called into discipleship by the Lord Jesus Christ, we understand more easily that such a community requires pastoral rather than strategic planning. In other words, it needs to pray and think together about the actions of the Body of Christ in a particular time and place rather than calculate resource inflows and outflows and the optimal resource allocation to achieve desired net revenue targets.

Bishops and diocesan leaders should see calls for strategic planning as the opportunity to educate and form lay leadership about the fundamental nature of the Church and the way in which the community needs to go about planning. Pretending that pastoral planning is strategic planning is misleading and can create confusion. It is better to be clear about what is needed, relevant, and consistent with the nature of the church.

SPECIAL PROJECTS

Because of the size and diversity of the modern diocese, there is a constant need for long-range planning for specific areas of diocesan operation. These might include planning projects for the diocesan newspaper, ministry personnel policies, health care ministries, campus ministries, policies regarding extern priests, strategic planning for the ministries of the diocesan curia, and leadership development processes. These projects might use a variety of planning methodologies and yet should be consistent with the pastoral planning process described here: central role of prayer, involvement of those directly affected by or working in the ministries, and clarification of mission and vision, focusing on the next best steps that would lead to the envisioned future. These projects also need a strong communication component to ensure that important constituencies are heard and are informed about the progress of the planning.

STAFFING FOR PLANNING

The bishop and his ministry have a special role to play in pastoral planning. Not only must he provide leadership and staffing to pastoral planning at the diocesan level but also, as we will see in the next chapter, he must provide significant resources to support regional planning. Support for pastoral planning at the parish and faith community level is typically part of the diocesan support for parish life, parish pastoral councils, and pastoral leadership. These types of resources and support are often part of the ongoing support from the diocese for parishes.

If a bishop agrees, as I argue here, that pastoral planning is an ongoing and life-giving process central to the life of the communion of disciples we call church, then he would provide for full-time, professionally competent staff to support diocesan, parish, and regional efforts. While consultants can be used to good effect in the design of a process, it is more cost-effective to use ongoing diocesan staff to support and implement the planning process. As with many aspects of life, it is not that pastoral planning is necessarily hard to understand, but it is difficult to implement because it requires a commitment over a significant period of time to facilitate the change in attitudes necessary for effective pastoral planning. If pastoral professionals and leaders think that the bishop is not approaching the planning task with the understanding and commitment necessary, they will be less likely to commit themselves to the change process.

Pastoral planning is not a thing that is done; it is a process that unfolds and thus requires ongoing support in terms of resources, staffing, and attention from the bishop.

Conclusion

This chapter has dealt with pastoral planning for the diocesan church. We essentially applied the generic pastoral planning process developed in chapter 4 with special attention to concerns and issues relevant to a diocesan church. In the preplanning phase we reviewed the following issues.

- Organizational: diocesan pastoral planning council or planning team
- Need for a path forward
- Question of focus: diocese, parishes, both
- Impact of diversity

In the application of the generic process, we gave special attention to the following elements.

- Diocesan websites
- Diocesan report formats
- Special relationships
  - Diocesan bishop
  - Finance council
  - Priests' council
  - Diocesan staff
  - Diocesan pastoral council

Finally, we addressed three important issues that often emerge in diocesan pastoral planning.

- Strategic planning or pastoral planning
- Special projects
- Staffing for planning

In the next chapter we turn to pastoral planning in regional groupings of parishes, a novel approach that U.S. and Canadian dioceses have created to deal with the practical realities of the Church in the United States and Canada.

Study Questions

1. Does your diocese have a diocesan pastoral council? If yes, how effective is it at pastoral planning? If no, what do you think are the reasons?
2. What would you add to or subtract from the diocesan information described in this chapter?
3. Do you tend to think of your bishop as an administrator or a pastor? What do you think are the differences between these two roles? How can one person be both at a high level of effectiveness?
4. In what ways can you distinguish pastoral planning from strategic planning?

CHAPTER 7

Implementation at the Regional Level

In this chapter we will discuss the application of pastoral planning at the intermediary level between the individual parish or faith community and the diocesan church. Since the mid-1990s the number of regional groupings of parishes in United States dioceses has been increasing. These groupings are part of the diocesan response to the decline in the number of priests. This is true both in dioceses where the population has been increasing as well as those with limited or no growth.

Dioceses have traditionally had vicariates, relatively large geographic subdivisions, so that certain administrative and canonical functions could be performed more efficiently. However, dioceses did not use vicariates as mechanisms for change and adaptation. These newly formed groupings exist to foster collaborative planning and action by parishes that hitherto were highly independent units of the diocese. While it is one thing for a parish to be included with neighboring parishes for the purpose of auditing sacramental records or providing Mass coverage during pastor illness or absence, it is quite another for a group of parishes to work together to plan their future and to collaborate in pastoral programs.

As a result, our discussion of pastoral planning in these situations will have two movements. The first will deal with the application of the generic pastoral planning process as we did with the parish and diocesan levels. The second will deal with the development of the infrastructure for collaboration required for regional planning. To accomplish this, we will first look at regional pastoral councils and their role in providing a structure for collaborative planning by multiple parishes. Because these structures rarely arise spontaneously and can often move in directions that make collaboration more rather than less difficult, we will next look at the special role of diocesan staff in creating and sustaining these regional collaborative structures.

Next, we will review the importance of providing a clear path forward for this type of planning. While it is not unusual for a parish or a diocese to engage in pastoral planning, regional groupings are typically approaching a new task and one that is often seen as having important and often negative consequences for the constituent parishes and faith communities. Finally, we will look at the application of the generic process to regional groups with a special focus on what has become known as configuration planning.

Formation of Regional Groups

While it is possible that a group of parishes could spontaneously come together to do joint pastoral planning and to collaborate in ministry, this is rarely the case. Typically the diocesan bishop has required this type of collaboration. Bishops in some dioceses have required such joint planning by some but not all parishes due to the impossibility of assigning priests as pastors to all parishes. Thus the bishop requires two or more parishes to work together to provide an acceptable solution to this "assignment" problem. Most clusters of parishes began their life in this fashion. Unfortunately this ad hoc planning, which may have been an appropriate and effective response to the assignment issue, is not very effective as a long-term planning response. As discussed earlier, effective pastoral planning processes are those that involve all parishes and faith communities rather than only those facing an immediate assignment problem.

The most effective approaches begin with a decision by the diocesan bishop to engage in comprehensive pastoral planning, that is, planning that involves all parishes. Since the objective is often to deal with a declining number of priests available for appointment as pastors, this decision to engage in comprehensive planning implies a commitment to planning in groups. This facilitates any ultimate clustering and combining of parishes to accord better with the number of priests available. There is no formula that could possibly determine the optimum composition of regional planning groups. Human judgment is required, guided by the following principles: proximity, current identity, existing relationships, maximum number of members, and the reaction of potential members.

While it might be tempting to create groups based on non-geographic variables, this should be avoided. The Church uses geography as an organizing principle for its faith communities; regional planning should respect this practice of the universal Church. While partnerships focused on specific pastoral issues can and should be forged along non-geographic lines, planning that can eventuate in the clustering or combining of parishes needs to begin with a geographically based group.

There is no perfect number of members of a planning group. Two parishes can comprise a group; this is often the case in small towns where there are two churches. While this seems like a simple group, it can often be the most challenging with which to work since any collaboration can easily be seen in won/lost terms. On the other hand, groups of seven or eight parishes can be very challenging to work with unless they are the parishes within a single small city or coherent geographic area like a single county or town division.

The preliminary grouping should be done by a small group of knowledgeable people who are familiar with the parishes of the diocese and who have no obvious vested interests. Groups should be developed for all the parishes at the same time, and each parish should be given the opportunity to react to its potential grouping. If a parish objects to its inclusion in a group, it needs to suggest an alternative, including the affirmation of the change by the members of the proposed group. To some extent this process can be arbitrary. If there is a pre-existing relationship among a set of parishes, then this relationship should be the basis for a grouping. If there is no relationship, then almost any grouping within reason will do since the creation of a working relationship will be the first order of business.

This process unfolds within the general context of an overall pastoral planning process for the diocese, and thus full and comprehensive communication will have informed parishioners and lay leaders about the need for and the process to be used in pastoral planning. Once the groups are finalized, the diocese should begin the process of organizing and structuring each group so that it is ready to begin pastoral planning. In all but the most highly staffed dioceses, the process of initiating planning requires a sequencing of groups over a multi-year period. Any attempt to change the reality of inter- parish relationships in a single year and with necessarily little involvement by diocesan staff only serves to undercut the planning effort.

Creation of Regional Pastoral Councils

Regional pastoral councils are composed of representative members from each parish or faith community. Typically four members represent each community: the pastoral leader and three lay members. At least one of the lay members should be a member of the parish pastoral council. If a parish or faith community has a significantly sized pastoral staff, one other lay member could be a staff member. Depending on the circumstances of each parish, religious or deacons can also be part of the four-member team. The three members from each community are selected by the pastoral leader and should meet the qualifications for members of the parish pastoral council members. In addition, these members should be open to new ideas, be held in respect by the community, be able to listen carefully to what others say, express themselves effectively, be prayerful, and be able to think about important issues rather than act out of emotional reactivity.

The process of constructing a regional pastoral council begins with a meeting of a diocesan staff person with the pastoral leaders of the parishes in the region. The bishop appoints a liaison to facilitate the formation of the group and to support it in the development of its pastoral plan. This meeting is the opportunity for the pastoral leaders to raise their questions and concerns about the planning process, their roles in it, and the desired outcome. In addition to the selection of the members from each parish, the pastoral leaders work together to discern the chair or likely co-chairs of the council. This is a key part of the process. Pastoral leaders know their own members well and also often know the leadership of the other parishes. Working together, they select and recruit a chair or co-chairs that have the experience and perspective to provide objective leadership to the process.

At the initial meeting of the regional council, the diocesan staff person provides an overview of the planning process and background information on the diocese and the parishes in the planning group. In addition, the bishop provides a written explanation of his expectations and the group's tasks and the issues to be addressed. The heart of his expectations will center on the number of priests likely to be available to each group over the next ten years and thus the implications for pastoral appointments. Demographic projections for Catholics and the general population over the same period should also be presented. Experience has demonstrated that groups doing pastoral planning must resolve the configuration issue before they can turn to consideration of more pastoral issues. As long as the fate of one's parish is uncertain, no amount of planning process can keep that issue from affecting almost all planning discussions. It is better to work out, affirm locally, and submit to the bishop a ten-year plan for the number of parishes or faith communities and their relationship. Once those issues are resolved, it is possible to turn to more pastoral issues within the newly evolving context.

There are many options for organizing a regional pastoral council. The format and style of the council should be compatible with the format and style of parish and diocesan pastoral councils. The most important difference between those typical structures and the regional councils is the authority with which they operate. The regional councils do not have autonomous, decision-making authority. They cannot make decisions that are binding on the constituent parishes and faith communities. They work on behalf of the member communities to pray and think together about the actions of the Body of Christ in the circumstances of today. Unlike the parish pastoral council, however, their perspective is one of the whole planning group. The regional council does pastoral planning for the collaborative ministry among all or some of the constituent parishes. They do not replace the parish pastoral councils but rather provide a collaborative focus.

Thus no decision of the regional council is binding on the member parishes unless the parishes all affirm the decision. Admittedly this is a high standard, but it is the only realistic way of building an infrastructure of trust on which collaboration can be built and difficult choices made. This is both sound social science and good theology. Long-term and lasting solutions to problems do not come from the imposition of solutions from a person or group with authority and power to force compliance. Short-term compliance may result, but long-term commitment and solutions arise when those involved come to terms with the need for action and design the solutions that respond to them.

The Christian notion of freedom of individual humans points us in the same direction. Our freedom as sons and daughters of God is not a license to do whatever we feel like, but rather gives us the ability to freely express in our decisions and actions the reality of God's spirit alive in us. The Church has long respected the principle of subsidiarity, in which decisions should be made at the level closest to those impacted by the decision. This is consistent with the principle that those affected by a decision should be consulted about the decision.

As a result, regional councils must operate with a rigorous consensus. In a sense the regional councils work on behalf of the constituent members to identify common issues and to provide creative and effective collaborative responses to them. Thus the work of the regional council depends on excellent communication and education, especially with pastoral councils of member parishes, which must affirm whatever the regional council develops. That unanimous affirmation is the basis for the regional council making its recommendation to the bishop and is the basis for the bishop's affirmation of the plan.

Role of Diocesan Staff

It is difficult to overestimate the challenge of beginning regional planning through groupings of hitherto independent and often competitive parishes and faith communities. Chris Argyris (See Appendix A) has made another important distinction between espoused values and values in action. It is relatively easy to espouse values, especially in response to attempts by those in power to change the "values of an organization." True and lasting change comes from changes in values in action, that is, those value assessments that we actually use in making choices about our behavior. Jesus well understood this dynamic. He was never dismayed by the Apostles' apparent inability to get his message. They would say all the right things, but when it got down to the reality of what he was called to do, they couldn't bring themselves to believe that and act on it. It was only after his death and resurrection and the emergence of the indwelling Spirit that they began to act on the values of Jesus. Jesus expressed this view when he said, "Not everyone who says to me 'Lord, Lord' will enter the kingdom of heaven, but only the one who does the will of my Father in Heaven" (Mt 7:21). Or as we read in the Letter of James, "Be doers of the word and not hearers only, deluding yourselves" (Ja 1:22).

The problem is not that we want to do the wrong thing, but that we are trapped in certain ways of seeing the world and resist the pain and work involved in changing our perspective. We know that a changed perspective will result in changed behavior, but it may be very difficult to tell exactly what changed behavior will look like. A bishop simply deciding that planning will take place, stating the problems to be addressed, convening a regional council, and empowering it to do pastoral planning will not be enough to change the fundamental values and assumptions that undergird our commitment to our individual parishes. The role of a diocesan staff liaison to the regional council—especially during the formative period—is to facilitate this new structure and the changes in perspective and trust it requires. Often this is in the context of difficult configuration decisions about which parishes will continue and which will be closed, combined, or merged.

The best way to understand the role of a diocesan liaison is to see him or her as a community organizer. She or he does not tell the council what to do or even necessarily how to go about its work but rather assists it in developing effective relationships with the other members and a sense of ownership of the work of the council. He or she provides a path forward (see below for the importance of this step), but much more importantly, the liaison works with both the formal and informal leadership of the group to assist them in keeping the council focused on the issues and the objectives presented by the bishop. She or he also serves an important information-sharing function. The liaison works with the council to produce a process and outcome that all members of the council and the constituent parishes own.

However, the planning liaison has one thing that a community organizer does not have: an agenda. The liaison is there to help the group respond to the bishop's issues and challenges. The planning group is not to create its own future separate from the reality of the diocese and its bishop but to resolve the issues he presents. Normally a liaison working with this agenda would find it impossible to establish a relationship of trust with the regional council. This is only possible if the bishop has made clear that he will accept any plan that responds fully and realistically to the planning issues and which is consistent with canon law, local diocesan legislation, and any other publicly announced policies and guidelines. Without this assurance, the planning liaison will always be seen as the person "from headquarters here to help us," which is code for someone from the bishop here to report on what we are doing and to make sure that we do what the bishop has already decided he wants done.

There is no one who has worked in this kind of role who has not dealt with people's certainty that there is a "secret plan" that makes all planning so much busy-work. "Just tell us what the bishop has decided so we can get on with whatever we need to do." This sentiment is not an irrational one. People have been manipulated by those in power, both within the Church and outside it, in exactly this way. They are suspicious, and they have a right to be. If this perception is to change, the bishop and the liaison he appoints must first be clear that there is no secret plan and that, within clearly specified boundaries, the regional councils are empowered to identify and resolve their pastoral issues. In a comprehensive process, the ways in which the first plans are developed and the way in which the bishop responds are critical to setting appropriate expectations and standards. If people see that, in fact, what they do does make a difference and that the bishop really does want them to create their own response to the issues, the liaison will have the room to operate as a community organizer with a declared agenda. If the early experience confirms people's preconceptions that there is a secret plan, no amount of organizational and communication skill will enable the liaison to operate effectively. The well has been poisoned and should be abandoned.

This is certainly a challenging task. The key ability is the skill at working with groups and individuals to achieve change when you do not have any real authority but must rely on one's own personal power and ability to influence. This is not the kind of work for someone who has issues of self-esteem or who feels that his or her own position and power must be constantly affirmed and highlighted. In his book *Leadership Without Easy Answers,* Ronald A. Heifetz provides a useful theoretical approach to exactly this kind of work. He especially focuses on situations in which one needs to exert leadership but has little or no formal authority, situations in which influence becomes more powerful than the ability to coerce. He uses the concept of a therapeutic holding vessel from counseling psychology.

People will engage in the hard work of achieving insight and changing behavior if the difficulty caused by their current perceptions and behavior is clearly problematic. However, if the problems are perceived as so great as to be overwhelming, a person will disengage from the therapeutic work. A therapist is constantly sensing this dynamic and adjusting the therapeutic environment to achieve movement toward health. At times the therapist is proactive in highlighting the problems caused by current insights and behavior but then eases the pressure as he or she senses that the line between therapeutic stress and overwhelming shutdown is about to be crossed. The trick is to hold the subject in this state of sufficient, but not too much, tension so that growth occurs.

A planning liaison engages in this same kind of behavior. The regional council would probably not even exist were it not for the stress and tension produced by the bishop's call to planning. The liaison must continue to call the council back to this work and its issues when it begins to stray or to pursue issues that will not lead to a plan that addresses the issues. At the same time, the liaison must be careful to understand when the difficulty of the issues is about to overwhelm the group and lead it into dysfunction and a failure to address the issues. This is especially the case when a regional council is dealing with a configuration question involving the destiny of one or more of the parish members. The liaison must constantly be tightening and then loosening the planning environment in the same way Heifetz describes the role of a therapist.

A person will find it difficult to maintain the calmness required for playing this role without deep personal emotional resources and without the active support of a management structure that understands and values this approach. Persons with fragile personalities and relatively shallow emotional resources will find it difficult to maintain their perspective when experiencing the opposition and anger of groups involved in deep planning processes. Even a person with sufficient personal resources will find it difficult to maintain this approach if he or she is constantly dealing with a management that wants results—and results with which it agrees—sooner rather than later. Such supervisors will often express this lack of support in words like the following: "I know all about that developmental process, but when are you going to get one of those parishes closed?"

Path Forward

While any process benefits from a clear path forward as a beginning point, regional planning requires one. Regional planning is a new activity, and it is essential to provide some way of approaching it so that people will engage in the initiation of the process. Convening groups, organizing leadership, setting forth challenges to be addressed, and then leaving people on their own sets up the planning group for failure and sets the stage for the imposition of a "secret plan" because "they couldn't deal with it." A genuine effort at regional planning will avoid this morass by providing a clear starting point and by supporting the planning with staff and resources. A clear starting point includes a statement of the need for planning, a set of criteria, guidelines, policies, canon laws to describe the area within which a planning solution will be found, projections of key planning variables, easily available resources, connections to other planning groups, deadlines/expectations, and a planning process. Let's look at each of these elements.

CLEARLY STATING THE NEED FOR PLANNING

This statement will come from the bishop and will clearly state the reasons for planning at the diocesan level as well as the planning issues each regional council is to address. This need not be an elaborate communication; in fact, simpler is better. A letter from the bishop to the leadership of the regional council, copied to all members and publicly available, is the best medium. This communication should make clear that this is a comprehensive process and that all parishes of the diocese are members of planning groups that will be engaging in collaborative pastoral planning. This communication should also focus on planning issues that the bishop wants each group to address. It is important that these issues are particular to each planning group and not simply generic statements of problems. They might include the following:

- A pastoral plan that will accommodate the numbers of priests likely to be available for ministry within the group over the planning period
- Any financial issues faced by parishes within the group
- Youth and young adult ministries
- Facility issues
- Number and timing of Masses (particularly if attendance indicates an issue)
- Catholic schools within the group
- Special ministry needs, for example, migrants, immigrants, campus, prison, and health.

In addition, the bishop should make available similar communication to other regional councils within the diocese so that all can see that the fundamental message is the same and that region-specific issues are also included. Finally, the letter should include some of the other information discussed below.

CRITERIA, GUIDELINES, POLICIES

One often hears in planning that "we need to think outside the box." This expresses a desire to think differently about the issues we face or about the possible solutions we create. It is a call for human inventiveness and creativity. However, it is essential to remember that in pastoral planning, there is a box. We are doing planning for a set of Roman Catholic faith communities in a specific diocese and in a specific civil society. It is essential that the bishop make clear the boundaries of this "box" so that participants know the arena within which they can exercise their creativity and innovative spirit. One diocese (Rochester, New York) has developed a relatively short list of what it calls planning constraints. Every pastoral plan must recognize and respect these policies that are based on universal Church law, local diocesan legislation, and interpretations of both.

- No priest will preside at more than three Sunday Masses each weekend (all references to "Sunday Masses" of course include Saturday Masses of anticipation).
- As a Eucharistic community, every parish must have a weekly Sunday Eucharist as long as this is possible and practical. There could be additional sites that are used for weekday Masses, weddings, and funerals. These will be properly seen as "chapels of ease" rather than parishes or parish Sunday worship sites.

Seasonal worship sites and / or seasonal Sunday worship schedules may be appropriate for areas impacted by seasonable changes in population.

- No priest pastor, priest administrator, or pastoral administrator will be assigned to more than three parishes. No parish will have more than three worship sites per assigned priest.
- A cluster of two or three parishes with a single pastor is not the norm in canon law. Typically, any cluster should be moving toward becoming a single canonical parish.
- Every parish, faith community, or worshipping community must meet the requirements and expectations appropriate to its nature. These will be based on the requirements of the universal church as well as local diocesan legislation.
- Sunday Celebration in the Absence of a Priest (SCAP) can be used only in short-term, emergency situations.

These are examples of the type of policies and constraints bishops should provide to regional planning. Another diocese may permit SCAP on a relatively regular basis because of local factors, such as the geographic isolation of parishes. The point is not that these are norms for such constraints but rather that constraints need to be realistic, clear, and unambiguous.

PROJECTING KEY PLANNING VARIABLES

Since much of regional planning is driven by the need of the diocese to respond to demographic changes with a reduced number of priests, it is important that each regional council be provided with the projections the diocese used to identify this problem. The diocese has determined that there is a current or projected problem, and it should provide the information and the resulting projections to each planning group. It is often tempting for diocesan officials to begin regional planning with a general sense of an increase or decrease in population (Catholic and general) and a decrease in the number of priests. Such a general approach, however, does not provide the urgency for planning discussed above and makes it all too easy to avoid the necessary planning work. Specific projections or estimates and the data on which they are based provide a solid basis for proceeding. These projections, especially of the number of priests, must take into account retirements, deaths, ordinations, and the number of extern priests, especially from foreign countries. Assignments of priests as pastors, parochial vicars, chaplains, and special workers should all be projected along with priests who are serving outside the diocese. These projections resolved to the regional level along with population estimates (see Percept described previously) provide the regional council with the projections it needs to do its work.

MAKING RESOURCES READILY AVAILABLE

Resources to support the regional planning process should be easily available to all those involved in the process. The most effective way to provide access to this resource is a diocesan website devoted to regional pastoral planning. In addition to all the planning resources mentioned earlier, the site should have a section organized by regional council. The section for each regional council should include the following:

- Parish and faith community members, with an information page for each
- Members of the regional council

- Profile of staffing appointed by the bishop: priests (pastors, chaplains, parochial vicars), permanent deacons, and pastoral administrators
- Summary of key sacramental data for the group
- Projections of priests and population
- Copy of bishop's letter initiating the planning process
- Interim progress reports
- Interim and final pastoral plans
- Letter from the bishop affirming the final plan
- Other information

This kind of information should be easily available to everyone. Nothing can distort a planning process like secrets and restricted formation. Nothing can empower people more than accurate and freely shared information.

CONNECTING WITH OTHER REGIONAL COUNCILS

The planning liaisons work to keep both formal and informal information flowing between regional groups. This is especially important as groups begin to develop new and creative approaches to planning issues. This information needs to be shared because it tends to expand the universe of possible solutions to problems. As soon as one council begins to consider a single parish with three worship sites, other groups can also begin to see that as a possible solution even if they initially would have thought it impossible. It is not so much that a solution developed by one group is adopted by other groups but rather that groups can be empowered as they hear the stories of other groups trying out new and novel approaches. The result is an entire system of innovating parishes and faith communities.

DEADLINES AND EXPECTATIONS

As long as the deadline is reasonable, every group works best when it knows that it faces a deadline for completion of its work. The bishop should include the deadline for affirmation in his initializing letter. Liaisons can make astute use of these deadlines to provide needed pressure to move a group to action. Often groups will have really completed the hard work but have not yet brought everything to conclusion. The existence of a deadline can provide that impetus.

The final part of the path forward is to provide an initial planning process that is the subject of the next sections. However, before we look at the application of the generic pastoral planning process to regional planning, it is necessary to discuss the special kind of planning that is often the focus and the reason for regional planning in the first place. So here we will look at a process for configuration planning.

Configuration Planning

The need for configuration planning varies by regions within the United States. Some regions face declining or stable population along with a decline in the number of priests. Other regions experience increasing population with the same decrease in the number of priests. In some isolated instances, the number of priests is increasing, although rarely at the same rate as the population. In almost all regions, the Catholic population mirrors the changes in the overall population. In some regions, however, immigration has produced increases in the Catholic population that exceed the increase in the general population. No matter what the case, however, all dioceses face questions about the number, relation, and location of parishes. Particularly when solutions involve the closure or combination of parishes, the most effective process to address these issues seems to be regional planning, in which parishes work together in groups to develop plans for the number and relationship of parishes.

These necessary adjustments are best accomplished when the very parishes that might be impacted do the planning directly. When a regional group faces these configuration issues, it is best to settle those issues before the work of pastoral planning begins. Until the exact form of the Body of Christ is clear, it is impossible to engage in meaningful planning about the actions of that body. If I am not sure that my parish will continue, it is very difficult for me to think about pastoral ministry needs. In fact, my responses and contributions to the ministry planning discussion may reflect my desire to continue my parish rather than a clear-eyed view of the pastoral needs within the region.

This section will address that challenge directly by describing a configuration planning process, which is consistent with the principles of the generic pastoral planning process but which proceeds in a somewhat different fashion. This configuration planning can be the opportunity to develop trusting and sincere relationships between people of multiple parishes even as it deals with the ultimate existence of these same parishes. Before we look at this process in detail, however, it will be helpful to describe what is meant by configuration.

A configuration plan is built around the number and relationship of parishes and the pastoral leadership models. Parishes/faith communities can exist in the following modalities:

- Single, stand-alone parish: This is the typical parish of forty years ago and is still the modal parish today. It consists of a single parish and is not linked in any meaningful way to other parishes.

- Single, stand-alone parish in collaborative relationships: This is like the parish above, but it has developed collaborative relationships, especially in pastoral ministry, with other neighboring parishes, similar parishes in other regions, or with parishes in need, typically in urban or rural areas.

- Cluster: This is composed of two or more parishes with a single pastoral leader. Such clusters were typically developed as responses to priest assignment challenges and were often seen as temporary. It has turned out in most dioceses that clusters have become permanent arrangements. Because of the multiplication of responsibility for a single leader with two or more parishes, most dioceses have begun to see these arrangements as part of the process of multiple parishes becoming a single parish. This does not happened overnight and should begin with the development of a single pastoral council for the multiple communities.

- Single parish with multiple worship sites/ churches: The merging of multiple parishes often creates a single parish with two or more churches. While this may be a transitional phase toward becoming a single parish with a single church, it may also be a permanent arrangement.

In addition to these parish models, there are five types of pastoral leadership that can be found in any of the parish types described above.

- Pastor: This is the traditional and normal situation in which a priest is appointed as pastor.

- Parochial Administrator: This is the appointment of a priest to lead a parish but without the canonical term required for a pastor. Parochial administrators have full responsibility for the parish and must be priests.
- Pastoral Administrator/Parish Life Coordinator: This is a person other than a priest assigned by the bishop to lead a parish and to be accountable to the bishop for the pastoral and temporal life of the parish. Dioceses have their own requirements for pastoral administrators; several require graduate theological education, extensive pastoral experience, and psychological assessment. The bishop can appoint lay men and women, male or female religious, and deacons to this role.
- Teams: Canon Law permits the appointment of teams of people to care for parishes. While it is desirable that any parish leadership be committed to a team approach, there are very few dioceses that have actually appointed teams to lead parishes.

These leadership models are combined with the parish modalities to provide a configuration plan for a group of parishes. Many details are also included, especially a timetable for implementation.

The following chart displays a configuration planning process for regional groupings of parishes and faith communities. The following is a discussion of each of these steps.

Configuration Planning Process Chart

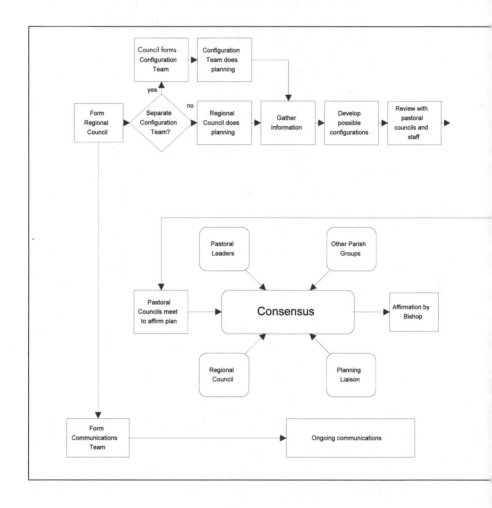

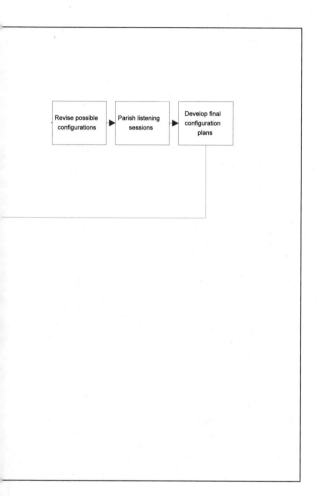

1. FORM REGIONAL OR GROUP COUNCIL

The process described above is used to form a regional council representative of the constituent parishes and faith communities. Each community is represented by its pastoral leader and three other members who are typically lay members.

2. FORM COMMUNICATION TEAM AND BEGIN ONGOING COMMUNICATION

To ensure ongoing and extensive communication, it is necessary to have a team of people who focus specifically on communication. The leadership of the regional council will shortly become very involved in the configuration issues and will not have the time or energy to divert attention to keeping members of the constituent communities informed. A dedicated team composed of people with experience in communication is the best way to ensure that a communication component is implemented effectively. It is almost always possible to find people with communication experience or expertise within the membership of the council. The diocesan liaison also provides important support and resources.

Once the team is assembled, it should begin its communication efforts immediately. Using the techniques described in the next chapter, the team will make sure that the regional council hears the needs and desires of the members of the communities and that the members of the communities are kept informed of the progress of the planning. This begins with communication of the membership, purpose, and timetable for this new council and how parishioners can keep up to date on the planning work.

3. ENTIRE COUNCIL OR CONFIGURATION TEAM?

The first decision of the council is whether to empower a team composed of members of the council to develop a draft configuration plan for consideration by the full council, or whether the full council should do the work. If a configuration team is used, its membership should include members from all constituent entities. It is usually good practice to have all pastoral leaders as members as well. It should neither appear to be true nor actually be true that the pastoral leaders are the ones doing the planning. Their involvement is essential but they must empower other members as well.

4. GATHER INFORMATION

Configuration planning then begins with the gathering of information as described in the parish process. The results should be shown both for each parish and for the group as a whole. A five-year time frame makes it possible to identify trends and changes. While each configuration process is different, there will generally be a focus on the following types of information:

- Number of registered households
- Average weekend Mass attendance
- Capacity of worship space
- Number of weekend Masses
- Percent of worship space utilized
- Baptisms
- Deaths
- Marriages
- Number of priests, deacons, and pastoral administrators assigned and types of assignments
- Special circumstances

The following charts are examples of the format for the presentation of reports from this basic data. These have been adapted from the report formats developed by the author at the Diocese of Rochester.

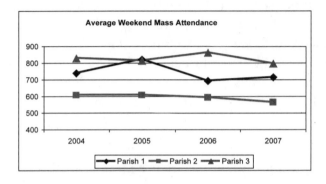

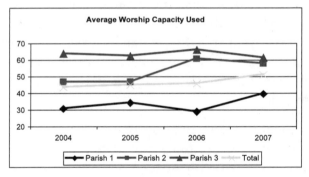

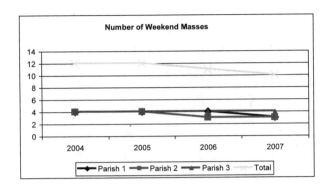

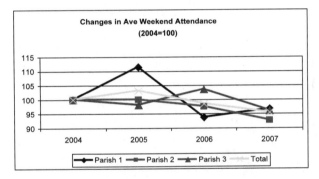

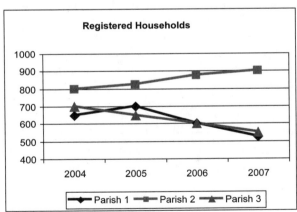

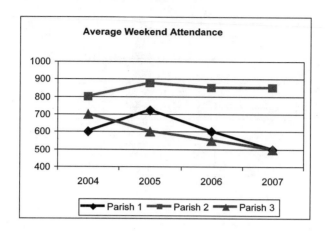

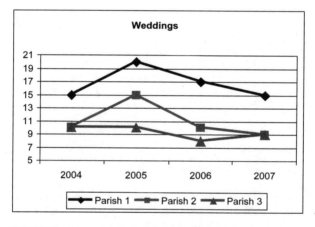

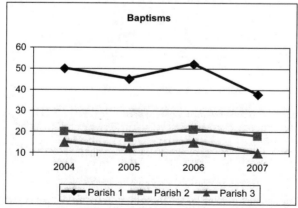

Also included in the initial information are the communication from the bishop regarding the projections of the number of priests likely to be available and the likely population projections for the regional planning group. This information, along with the policy constraints provided by the bishop, forms the boundaries within which the planning will proceed. Depending on the direction of the planning, the group may require fairly detailed information about the physical facilities of the constituent members. The diocesan office responsible for physical assets of the diocese can typically provide this. In any event, such detailed information is not necessary at the beginning of the process.

A critical piece of information at this stage of the process is provided by the planning liaison: planning scenarios. The planning liaisons have the broadest view of the planning process, diocesan needs, and the work of other planning groups both inside and outside the diocese. They know that often groups will shy away from more extreme responses to configuration issues because they involve difficult feelings and often can disrupt the emerging unity of the planning group. At the same time, planning liaisons know how important it is to expand the universe of possible planning responses. A premature narrowing of the options because of the awkwardness or difficulty of dealing with more extreme options can reduce a planning effort to ineffectuality and lead to a failure to deal realistically with the issues the bishop has placed before the group. Thus it is important that the planning liaison provide the group with two or three possible configuration scenarios that respond to the issues before the group.

Entities		Priests		Other Staff		Ratios	HH	ATT	CAP
Parishes	4	Pastor	2	Deacons	4		2589	2990	1950
Colleges	2	Administ.	0	Pastoral Admin	1	Parish Ratio	647	748	488
Hospitals	2	Par Vicar	0			Deacon Ratio	647	748	488
Prisons	0	Sac Min	1	**Current Priests 2007**	**3**	**Cur Priest Ratio**	863	997	650
Migrant	0	Chaplain	0	**Projected Priests 2008-12**	**3**	**2012 Priest Ratio**	863	997	650
Other	1	Other	0	**Projected Priests 2013-17**	**2**	**2017 Priest Ratio**	1295	1495	975
Total	**9**	**Total**	**3**	Largest Worship Space	700	07 Min. Masses in Largest W.S.			6.1

Special Circumstances:

Comments:

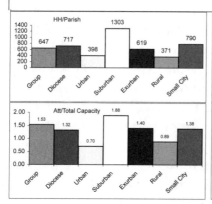

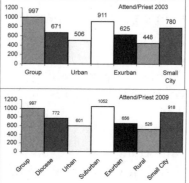

				Suburban				
M	**B**	**F**	**W**	**Priest**	**D**	**O**	**E**	**Tot**
15	143	104	39	Priest1	1			
3.75	36	26	10	Priest2	1			
4	36	26	10	Priest3		1		
5.00	48	35	13					
5.00	48	35	13					
7.50	72	52	20					
2007 ATT/CAP	1.53							
				Total	2	1	0	3
				D	Diocesan			
				O	Order			
				E	Extern			

KEY	
HH	Registered Households
ATT	Average Weekend Mass Attendance
CAP	Capacity of all churches
M	Weekend Masses
B	Yearly Baptisms
F	Yearly Funerals
W	Yearly Weddings
W.S.	Worship Space
ATT/CAP	
Ratio of total capacity of worship spaces to the total weekend attendance. This is a measure of the demand for worship space that can be used to make comparisons among different groups.	

Min. Masses in largest worship space is calculated using an average of 70% capacity used and current weekend attendance.

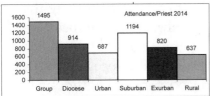

Attendance/Priest 2014

Group	1495
Diocese	914
Urban	687
Suburban	1194
Exurban	820
Rural	637

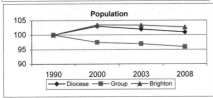

Population

1990 2000 2003 2008

— Diocese — Group — Brighton

It must be clear that these do not constitute the "secret plan" but rather are possible responses to the issues. Liaisons know that sometimes it is easier for a group to express disagreement and even anger with a liaison than with another member of the group. The use of scenarios is a method for getting "parking lot" conversations about solutions into the meeting where all participants can discuss and review them in an open, trusting, and respectful manner.

5. DEVELOP POSSIBLE CONFIGURATIONS

Using the information of the previous step, including possible scenarios, the planning group works to develop potential configuration responses. The planning liaison plays a key role in facilitating this process by bringing the fruits of his or her experience with other groups to bear. He or she is also constantly increasing or decreasing the tension of the planning environment to move the process forward without crossing the line of disillusionment and withdrawal. This is not the time to push through to a single configuration response unless there is a clear consensus. Configuration plans deal with the number and location of parishes, the inter-relationship of parishes, the number of worship spaces, number of Masses, and pastoral leadership models (pastor, pastoral administrator, or parish life coordinator). At this stage, the ideal situation is to have two or three options with which to gain reaction from the member communities.

6. REVIEW WITH PASTORAL COUNCILS AND PARISH STAFFS

While a communication team has been keeping the pastoral councils and parish staffs (if any) informed about the progress of the planning, it is important to make a special and focused effort to obtain their reaction to the first results of configuration planning. Using the two or three options developed in the previous step, the regional council hosts a session in which the pastoral councils and staff members of all constituent members meet to hear the results of the early work and to provide comment and reaction. This is the first time that the planning group will get an idea of the acceptability of its proposals. The use of multiple possibilities is essential lest the members of the councils and the staff think that a single option indicates decisions have already been made.

7. REVISE POSSIBLE CONFIGURATIONS

Based on the input from parish pastoral councils and staffs, the planning group revises, sometimes drastically, its possible configurations. Perhaps it is now possible to begin to move toward a single recommendation. If this is the case, then the group should do that. However, it is still useful to have options to present to the membership of the parishes in the next step. The group may need to do additional research and gather more information in order to answer questions raised in the review with parish pastoral councils and staffs. The planning council may also need to do additional research to support more sophisticated or innovative configurations.

8. PARISH LISTENING SESSIONS

All through the process, a communication program has been keeping the parishes and their members informed of the progress and milestones of the planning. Thus the announcement of comprehensive parish listening sessions should not come as a surprise since people should have at least a general idea of the scope of the planning. The listening sessions are best held on a parish-by-parish basis. All members are invited to attend and there may be multiple sessions to make sure that all are heard from.

After a brief review of the configuration options, usually by a lay member of the planning group representing that parish, people are invited to provide their reactions, comments, and criticism of the proposed plan(s). The members of the planning group representing the parish, including the pastoral leader, should be in attendance. It is important, however, for these members not to engage in argumentation with those who object to the proposed plans. In fact, the whole approach should be one of identifying strengths and weaknesses rather than focusing on approval/disapproval. It should be made clear that nothing has been decided and that the purpose of the session is to learn about the strengths and weaknesses of the proposals so that the planning group can improve its work. At the same time, it needs to be made clear that a plan must be produced, affirmed, and presented to the bishop because he has decided that this is how he wants the diocesan church and its parishes to deal with these issues.

Careful notes of the comments and reactions should be taken. People should be encouraged to provide additional input in writing, e-mail, or personal communication with the parish's representative to the group. The written record of the responses will be made available so that everyone understands that this is a transparent process.

9. DEVELOP FINAL CONFIGURATION RECOMMENDATIONS

Using all the information and reaction gathered above, the planning group devises its final configuration recommendation. There is no particular form for these documents. A review of various diocesan web sites will disclose a variety of approaches, each of which fits the local situation. Once the final recommendation is completed, the planning group works to achieve a consensus that this is the recommendation they want to send to the parish pastoral councils for affirmation. This consensus is reached when each member indicates that he or she can support the proposal with his or her parish pastoral council. If this is not possible, work on the proposal continues until it reaches that point of consensus without any loss of effectiveness. The planning liaison plays a key role in providing guidance when necessary about the extent to which a proposed formulation will be seen by the bishop as effectively addressing the issues. Often the planning liaison can assist a group by helping them stage implementation so that parish communities have the time to prepare properly.

10. PASTORAL COUNCILS MEET TO REVIEW AND AFFIRM

In a well-implemented process, this affirmation should be routine since no one is being surprised. Discussion has been extensive, and input has been both heard and utilized. The final recommendation may be a painful one, but all involved should agree that, as unpleasant as it is, the plan is a rational response to issues that must be addressed and that it is workable enough that people can commit to implementing it. Sometimes this final step requires more process as described in the next section.

11. CONSENSUS

In the end, many components of the parishes and the group have to agree with and affirm the plan. Often this requires a continuous process of adjustment and review that involves pastoral leaders, parish groups, regional council, the planning liaison, and perhaps others. The liaison can facilitate this process and help it move toward conclusion by calling people back to the goal and the deadline set by the bishop. The draft–response–redraft cycle described earlier is useful in this process.

12. AFFIRMATION BY THE BISHOP

Once the plan is completed and affirmed by the pastoral leaders and pastoral councils, it is submitted to the bishop. He and his staff review the plan and respond in writing with an affirmation of the direction of the plan. This should be a straightforward process since the planning liaison will have kept the bishop informed of the direction of the plan and will have provided any indications of non-acceptance to the planning group. It is important that the plan be affirmed as long as it addresses the configuration issue realistically and stays within the guidelines provided at the beginning of the process. The bishop and his staff should avoid the temptation to disapprove a plan that they feel is not the best one, that is, the one they would have devised. As long as the requirements are met, the plan and the process that produced it should be respected.

This respect is important not only because it establishes the credibility of the process for the other parishes and faith communities that will go through the process but, more importantly, because the parishes and their leaders must implement the plan. If they feel a strong sense of ownership of the plan, and if the process has produced effective working relationships and trust, they are in an excellent position to invest the effort required to make any reconfiguration plan work. If their work is rejected and another put in its place, even if the replacement plan is objectively better, they will focus their energy on the process by which the plan was imposed rather than on the implementation of the plan itself.

In effect, a bishop who leads his diocese in this kind of planning commits himself to the process as well. The bishop always retains his power and authority; he cannot delegate it to others in the same way that corporate executives do. However, trusting in the Spirit that enlivens the Church as the People of God, a bishop can willingly and gracefully constrain the exercise of his authority in light of the solid contribution of the people of the diocese. Without this willing constraint, configuration planning will eventually become the manipulation that many people fear it would be at the beginning.

Regional Pastoral Planning

Once the configuration issue is resolved and (if necessary) a reconfiguration plan is in place, it is timely for a regional group to begin pastoral planning as described in the generic process. The composition of the regional group can become quite messy as a result of reconfiguration. A regional group of three parishes may reconfigure as a single parish with three churches and campuses. In that case, the regional group does pastoral planning as described for implementation at the parish level in chapter 5. In other cases, for example, a regional group of five parishes may reconfigure into two clusters: one with two parishes and one with three. Each of the clusters would engage in pastoral planning as described in chapter 5, with the obvious adjustments required for clusters. The regional group itself would proceed to look at regional issues as described next. Until we can be clear about the number of parishes and their relationships, we cannot proceed with pastoral planning at the parish, cluster, or regional level. Once that situation is clarified, however, regional planning can proceed.

MISSION AND VISION STATEMENTS

At the regional level, the generic planning process is implemented in a straightforward way. There are really only a few adjustments. First, the regional group will need to develop a mission and vision statement that is more than the sum of or some combination of the parish mission and vision statements. Doing this can often end up with mission statements that resemble the set of magnetic words on the refrigerator: You can keep rearranging the words without adding meaning and often without changing the meaning. The regional council should approach this beginning of the pastoral planning cycle anew and should use the process and forms described for writing a mission and vision statement from scratch.

GATHERING INFORMATION

The information for the regional group is the same as that collected and analyzed for a single parish or cluster, but combined to show a picture of the group and to enable comparisons with other groups. The same processes and forms described in chapter 5 can be used, with obvious adjustments for multi-member regional groups.

FOCUSING INFORMATION AND IDENTIFYING ISSUES

The regional level requires adjustments at this point in the process. Ideally parishes engaging in a regional process have already been doing parish pastoral planning and thus have a good sense of their own information and their hopes and fears that arise from that. They have used these to identify issues and concerns, and perhaps have identified some goals in line with these. Each constituent member of the regional group brings this information to the group level and together the representatives look for common concerns and issues that can form the basis for collaborative action. The plan is built on goals that address common concerns and issues better or more cost-effectively than would be the case if each parish addressed issues individually.

From this point on, the regional planning addresses collaborative pastoral activity. Each parish is engaging in pastoral planning and activity in its own right along with the group process. The remaining steps of the generic process apply:

- Engagement of the Parish Communities
- Revision and Finalization of Mission, Vision, Issues/Opportunities
- Development of Goals
- Development of Objectives
- Development of Action Steps
- Engagement of the Parish Communities Part II
- Affirmation
- Implementation and Assessment

For regional pastoral activities, the regional council provides the point of accountability for the regional plan. It has no authority over the parishes other than that implied by the parishes' affirmation of the plan and their agreement to work together in implementation. The planning liaison plays an essential role in continuing to work with the regional group as it goes about implementing the plan.

Conclusion

In this chapter we reviewed pastoral planning at the intermediate or regional level. This is the newest and often most confusing setting for pastoral planning. It calls on parishioners to change their focus away from their parish and toward collaborative relationships with other parishes.

We reviewed the techniques for forming regional groups, including the composition of membership. The infrastructure for collaboration is built around a regional pastoral council that is representative of the constituent members of the planning group. Pastoral leaders play an important and empowering role in the formation process. Perhaps the most important aspect of regional councils is their authority—or really their lack of independent authority. The work of the council has standing only to the extent that the pastoral leaders and pastoral councils of the member entities affirm its work and to the extent that the bishop does the same. This affirmation by the member entities must be unanimous. An operational consensus is the mode of governance of these regional councils. This places a premium on effective process and astute leadership.

We then reviewed the central role of diocesan staff, specifically a diocesan planning liaison. This person works as a community organizer with a clearly declared agenda. This is possible only to the extent that the bishop has been explicit about the planning objectives and the constraints, or "box," within which the plan must fit. A therapeutic concept borrowed from Ronald Heifetz was suggested as a model for the work of a planning liaison. A clear path forward is essential to this type of planning. The elements of such a path forward are the following:

- Clear statement of the need for planning
- Set of criteria, guidelines, policies, canon law requirements
- Projections of key planning variables
- Easily available resources
- Connection to other regional councils
- Deadlines and expectations

The final piece of an effective path forward is a workable planning process. Because of the nature of regional planning, we reviewed a process for configuration planning that included the following steps:

- Form regional council
- Form communication team and begin ongoing communication
- Use entire council or form a configuration team
- Gather information
- Develop possible configurations
- Review with pastoral councils and parish staffs
- Revise possible configurations
- Host parish listening sessions
- Develop final configuration recommendations
- Review and affirmation by parish pastoral councils
- Reach consensus
- Seek affirmation by the bishop

Once configuration planning is completed and moving toward implementation, it is possible for the regional grouping to begin a pastoral planning process based on the generic process described in chapter 4. We discussed the major differences in the areas of mission, vision, gathering information, focusing issues, and identifying goals. The regional council submits its recommendations to the member parishes and then to the bishop for affirmation. It then serves as a point of accountability for the implementation of the collaborative plan and begins the planning cycle again as the five-year period comes to a close.

Study Questions

1. Do you currently have "infrastructure" for collaboration with other parishes and faith communities? If yes, describe it. If no, what are the ways in which you can create it?

2. The role of a diocesan liaison to regional planning groups was described as a community organizer with a declared agenda. Does that definition make sense to you? How would you define this role? What kind of person should a liaison be in terms of education, experience, and personal characteristics?

3. Configuration planning is a special type of pastoral planning. Do you think your parish or faith community needs to engage in configuration planning? If so, how do you think it can best go about it?

4. As you think about your situation, are there pastoral concerns and issues that seem to cry out for collaborative ministry? What are they, and how difficult do you think it would be? How difficult do you think it should be?

CHAPTER 8

Communication

At many points in our discussions of the generic planning process and its application to parish, diocesan, and regional planning, as well as in our discussion of configuration planning, we noted the importance of effective communication. We deferred a discussion of the approach to and techniques of communication to this chapter. The understanding of communication and the ways in which it can play a role in planning do not vary in any material way across the different planning levels. What is clear about planning at all levels is that excellent and thoughtful communication is an essential ingredient for a process that advances the mission of a community of disciples. This is especially true when dealing with difficult and painful challenges.

In this chapter, we will first discuss the nature of communication and then consider some of the aspects of effective communication gleaned from experience. As we will see, communication is both receiving and transmitting information. So we will review some of the ways in which we can be effective listeners. Then we will look at the elements of a communication plan: key audiences, key messages, media, and implementation.

What Is Communication?

Communication is the process by which information is exchanged between two or more people. This is a simple definition for what can easily become a very complex phenomenon. Both the type of information and the number and type of people can vary greatly. One spouse telling the other about vacation plans is a fairly straightforward process. The information is simple and only two people are involved. Communication is face-to-face and thus does not require any medium of communication. Increasing the amount and complexity of information and the number of recipients results in a potentially difficult and tricky communication process. For example, consider a cousin organizing a week-long family reunion for an extended family of seventy-five members! The information is more complex and will change as the plans themselves change. Face-to-face communication will turn out to be less effective than more standardized written communication. Even the emotional content of the communication will have an impact on the process: who currently likes or dislikes whom, the shifting alliances within the family, those who would like to make the decisions, those who would like to go to a different place, those who like to engage in a different activity, and, of course, those who truly don't want to have anything to do with the whole thing.

Communication is both multi-dimensional and interactive. Rarely is the information a simple fact. Information can be complex, freighted with emotion and feeling, contradictory, conditional, persuasive, declarative, and/or hortatory. To complicate the process even further, communication is interactive. The content and method of communication is always affected by the response, both rational and emotional, of the recipient. This response cycle is continuous and often subtle. This is the reason why conversations seem to take on a life of their own and end up with language and topics unanticipated and unintended at the beginning of the communication exchange.

A communication exchange is accurate to the extent that the received information is the same as the transmitted information. While there are many other dimensions of communication, the heart of effective communication is this simple insight. The information communicated should be clear, unambiguous, direct, and phrased at a level and with a vocabulary appropriate to the recipient. The recipient should attend to the communication exchange with the purpose of receiving and understanding the information as intended by the transmitter. Most communication problems arise from the recipient prematurely processing the information to determine agreement/disagreement as well as the appropriate response, rather than waiting to make sure the message is fully and clearly understood.

Transmitted information is subjectively true if it accurately depicts the knowledge, attitude, and perspective of the transmitter. It will be objectively true if the information content corresponds to external reality. It is possible for a communication to be subjectively true but objectively false. I can be clear about what I think about a situation, but I may have misunderstood the situation. I can understand a situation but be so confused about it that I have a difficult time being clear in my communication. And, of course, I can both misunderstand the situation and be confused about it. The problem, especially for highly verbal people, is that the communicator often is not really clear about his or her knowledge, attitude, or perspective and often works this out in the process of communication. Given the highly complex and interactive nature of communication, this can result in a slightly different formulation with each communication. As composition teachers have taught us all, you must be clear about what you think before you can write clearly. We can also add that before you can be clear about how you think about a subject, you need to accurately understand the subject. When a communication exchange deals with important and potentially disturbing information, it is especially important for the transmitter to work out the content of the message and to choose words and vocabulary appropriate to the audience and the tone of the communication. For this reason, a draft–review–redraft cycle is the best way to achieve a communication that is subjectively and objectively true. The use of a set of knowledgeable people who will review the proposed communication and provide feedback and reaction is invaluable to an accurate, true, and effective communication exchange.

Before we look at some techniques of effective communication, we need to remind ourselves of one other basic insight. An information exchange rarely begins from scratch. The target recipients have typically already had some involvement with the topic and also have some needs for information. The information they desire may or may not be the information the transmitter desires to transmit or may not be the most important information to be transmitted. If intended recipients do not have their need for information satisfied, they are much less likely to attend to a communication exchange with only information intended by the transmitter. If I have a need to hear z, and the communicator spends time and effort transmitting A through Y but never mentions z, I will not only have my need for z frustrated, but I will also begin to doubt the credibility of the communicator and begin to invent all sorts of explanations for the failure to address the issue important to me. If a planning process begins with a gathering of parishioners and with an agenda focused on planning issues and processes, but the people gathered have a need to hear about the response to clergy sexual abuse, the better communication process will provide for some time to deal with that issue in order to move on to the agenda at hand.

In summary, communication is listening to others and transmitting information to others. The essence of effective communication is to listen to the needs, issues, and concerns of the target audience and to transmit information that responds to those needs, as well as to transmit information that calls an audience to previously unrealized issues or processes.

The Basics of Communication

There are eight rules of thumb about effective communication. Even if one cannot follow all the communication strategies discussed later in this chapter, one can be an effective communicator by keeping the previous discussion in mind and then focusing on these simple bits of advice gleaned from years of practical experience in communication.

DURING TIMES OF CHANGE, IT IS IMPOSSIBLE TO OVERCOMMUNICATE.

This is often difficult for those in positions of authority and in charge of a change to appreciate. They can tend to feel that once they have communicated the change, their communication work is done. In fact, the communication needs to be repeated in different formats and through different media. What is at stake here is not the accuracy of the communication but the emotional bond between those leading the change and those impacted by the change. The more communication between those leading and those impacted by the change, the more those impacted can act out of clear thinking rather than emotional reactivity resulting from a sense of abandonment and dismissal of their needs. During times of change, when those in leadership positions think they have communicated enough, they should redouble their communication. Seventy times seventy may not be too much.

REPETITION IS THE HEART OF EFFECTIVE COMMUNICATION.

Even when change is not at the forefront of people's consciousness, repetition is the key to effective communication. Particularly in a media-drenched culture like twenty-first-century America, there is a constant battle for attention. The fact that "no one reads the bulletin" should be understood as people behaving rationally rather than irresponsibly. There are so many messages bombarding us that we select those that seem most important, relevant, or entertaining. Realistically, it is not the importance of the content of the message that determines the attention people give it. Even with all the creativity and resources of modern commercial media, advertisers understand that repetition is the key to breaking through the barriers to attention. While pastoral leaders do not have these tools at hand, they do have a platform to which people attend. Hence, it is important that they repeat key messages from that platform. This repetition may well become boring for the transmitter, yet the repetition must be continuous if it is to capture people's attention.

PROVIDE SMALL BITES RATHER THAN THE WHOLE STEAK.

Those in positions of authority and leadership would like to think that a single comprehensive communication, a pastoral letter, for example, is the best way to get a message across. Clearly such a formal statement is important, and its very formal nature captures many people's attention. However, the effective communication of the messages within it will only take place through many smaller messages consistently communicated over a period of time. Because of the limited amount of time people have to attend to messages, long and comprehensive messages, no matter how well expressed, will not hold the attention of the intended audience. Skillfully dividing a complex message into shorter and simpler messages is the key to communication.

OPPORTUNISTIC COMMUNICATION CAN SUPPORT A FORMAL COMMUNICATION PROCESS.

No matter how well we design a communication plan, we will encounter opportunities for communication that we did not anticipate. Taking advantage of these opportunities is an important way of supporting and reinforcing the planned communication. When a pastoral leader is called on to provide a prayerful beginning to a meeting of a ministry, he or she can work in one of the major communication themes, not as a conscious planning discussion but as a natural consequence of the ministry in question. For example, if one of the communication messages is to focus people on the opportunities for collaborative ministries with neighboring parishes, an opening prayer for a social justice ministry team could include a prayer for the members of the social justice ministry teams of the other parishes or even a specific mention of a ministry of one of the parishes. Pastoral and ministry leaders need to be alert to opportunities to naturally reinforce communication messages.

INFORMAL COMMUNICATION HAS A DISPROPORTIONATE IMPACT ON RECEIVERS.

While our communication plan will focus on formal communication, we know that informal, face-to-face communication often has a more powerful impact on recipients of the information. At its worst this is gossip; at its best it is freely flowing information in a system in which there are few if any secrets. In almost every system, there are secrets and restricted information. This restriction gives rise to a distinction between those who are in the know and those outside the circle of influencers. In fact, what happens is that people who aren't really in the know begin to act and talk as though they are. Since information is restricted, there is no effective way to determine who knows and who does not. The result is a richly developed system of gossip and rumors.

Effective communication will make use of both the formal and informal communication channels in a way that does not enhance the position of those who deal in rumors and gossip. In every system, there are those to whom others look to provide cues about how to understand what is happening. It is important that an effective communication system identifies these people and ensures that they are well informed about the content and process of planning. While the thrust of an effective communication process democratizes information as discussed below, it is important that those who have been dealers in informal information be provided accurate information. This should not be done in a way that creates secrets since that will only perpetuate a system of influence based on information power.

PEOPLE ARE NOT AT THEIR BEST WHEN THEY ARE SURPRISED.

This requires little elaboration. If we reflect on our reactions when we find ourselves surprised by events or people, we find that we become defensive and begin to respond to the person who surprised us rather than to the content of the information. If the intent of a planning process is to engage the best thinking of all those involved, advance notice and especially, advance copies of material will become routine.

THE TRUTH WILL SET US FREE, EVEN IF THE TRUTH IS TROUBLESOME.

The type of planning described in this book is based on a simple premise: everyone should have access to the best information that is relevant to the work at hand. Systems that restrict information tend to create inequalities and thus, dysfunction. In hierarchical systems, there is always the temptation to promote a planning process with the final decision firmly in the hands of a hierarch. As has been described above, this is part of the Catholic tradition and can easily accommodate the planning process described here. What is important is that the process used by the decision maker should be transparent and the information used visible and easily available to all those involved in the process. Without this transparency there is the danger that the judgment of the decision maker will be substituted for that of those involved in the planning since they do not have access to the same information as the decision maker.

There is almost never a downside to the free flow of accurate information throughout an organization. It empowers those closest to the issue to make effective decisions, and it encourages decision makers to develop a stronger sense of accountability to the people they serve.

FEEDBACK THAT MAKES A DIFFERENCE IS CRUCIAL.

Throughout this book and especially this chapter on communication, we talk about feedback. One of the central dynamics is the draft–reaction–redraft cycle for the creation of documents and plans. Reaction from people is essential to the process. However, feedback does not relieve those involved in the planning process from exercising their own judgment for the benefit of the whole. What is significant about feedback is that it must be recognized and taken into account. A development process that simply includes all feedback results in a jumble of everyone's ideas. A process that excludes feedback from others results in the views of only one person becoming the norm. The middle way is for feedback to be recognized and taken into account in ways that people can see. While it is not necessary to give equal weight to the content of all feedback, it is necessary to acknowledge all feedback and to provide a description of how the feedback was understood and how it was used in the process or why it was not used. Feedback does not eliminate the need for decision making by those in leadership positions, but it does require them to provide their assessment of feedback, a description of how it was or was not used, and an explanation of that decision.

Techniques for Listening

Since listening to others even before we begin to transmit information is a key to effective communication, we need to look at ways in which we can truly listen to others. In this section, we will discuss active listening, focus groups, listening sessions, surveys, and unsolicited input.

ACTIVE LISTENING

As long as we are conscious, we constantly hear external sounds. Listening implies that we are purposefully attending to those sounds and attempting to understand their content. When we listen to other people speaking, we can easily be distracted by competing sounds, our own unrelated thoughts, and our response to what we are hearing. The first is an environmental issue. The second is

daydreaming. The third is the result of our own thought processes as we prepare to respond to the other person. Any of
these will interfere with our ability to listen to other people
and understand what they are communicating in terms of
both content and affect.

Active listening requires a full and focused attention on
the other person with the intent of understanding as fully as
possible the content and affect of what he or she is saying.
While one may be in a position that requires a response, it
is important that one has a good grasp of what the other
was saying. Active listening typically means that the listener
repeats what he or she has heard the other person say and
then asks checking questions to make sure this is accurate
and to clarify any issues or nuances where there might still
be misunderstanding. Active listening can also involve the
emotional characterization of what was said if that is clear.
Hearing anger in a person's voice is part of the communication and stating that in an objective way along with the content provides validation to and empathy with the speaker.

Once we are clear about the content of the message, we
are in a position to provide a response if that is necessary
and appropriate. More often than we realize, however,
people do not need a response but rather recognition of what
they said and how they feel. If a response is appropriate, it
should be complete, direct, and to the point. If we do not
know the answer to a question or simply do not know how
to respond, it is better to admit that and promise to provide
a response at a later time. While external distractions and
daydreaming can obviously prevent active listening, the real
problem is trying to listen to another and think about our
response at the same time. Often this is an attempt to defend
our position and convince the other person to accept our
position. In that process of thinking about what we are going
to say, we do not actively listen to others and thus run the
risk of missing both their content and affect. The resulting

communication from us can then make things worse rather than better.

The best way to become an active listener is to take a learning stance as we listen, particularly if the content and affect are difficult or attacking. If a listener focuses on learning as completely as possible the message of the other without immediate reference to its impact on the listener or the response to be made, it becomes easier to listen actively. This is especially important when we are advocating a position opposed by the communicator. If we can listen to that small voice in the back of our heads that says, "No matter how convinced I am of our position, I might be wrong," then we can listen to the other person and hope to learn more about the issue and perhaps improve our own position.

FOCUS GROUPS

A focus group is a technique adapted from marketing research. It was originally developed to identify underlying emotional reactions to products or potential products. In a marketing setting, it is implemented by an objective third party and is videotaped so that the client can not only read the content of reactions but also read the affect in both language and body positions. In the free-flowing discussion of a focus group, implementers are alert for striking words or phrases participants use to express their feelings and attitudes. Focus groups have been highly effective in helping marketing campaigns devise advertising and communication programs that address potential customers on many levels, as well as in devising or redesigning the products or services themselves.

This methodology has been adapted in pastoral planning to elicit and record participants' reactions to pastoral issues and possibilities. Focus groups are not designed to arrive at any definitive conclusion but rather to provide a setting in which people feel free to express their experience, feelings, and attitudes about relevant pastoral issues. They are especially useful in listening to parishioners, pastoral staff, pastoral leaders, and lay ministry leaders to uncover pastoral issues and potential responses to those issues.

Since most dioceses and almost all parishes cannot afford the cost of a professionally implemented focus group as described above, the methodology has been adapted. Each focus group has between seven and twelve participants. A group can be either homogeneous or heterogeneous. A homogeneous group is composed of only pastoral leaders, parishioners, parish staff, seniors, young adults, youth, or whatever other classification seems relevant. Such groups are especially effective when there are big status differentials within a heterogeneous group. For example, if pastors and youth were in the same group, it might be difficult for the youth to fully express their feelings and attitudes. On the other hand, a homogeneous group can tend more easily toward "groupthink" rather than moving into unexplored territory. A heterogeneous group will be more complex and will draw upon a richer diversity of experience and perspective.

Each group has a facilitator and a recorder. The facilitator serves the group by ensuring that all participate and that a few individuals do not dominate the discussion. The facilitator needs to be aware that the purpose is not to arrive at a conclusion or consensus. The purpose of a focus group is to achieve the fullest possible expression of the thoughts and attitudes of the participants without any attempt to assess or judge those thoughts or attitudes. This can be particularly difficult if a pastoral leader is a member of the group and feels compelled to defend decisions. It is absolutely necessary that such defensiveness and argumentation not become a part of the focus group process.

The facilitator will lead the group through the open-ended questions posed to the focus group and will guide the discussion so that all participate and all questions are considered. No focus group should run more than ninety minutes, and this expectation should be clearly stated at the beginning. The recorder captures the essence of the responses of the members and is especially alert to words or phrases that are striking or seem to sum up the feelings and attitudes of the group. These notes are best taken on a lap top computer with the results shared widely and freely.

It is essential that the focus group consider open-ended questions designed to give participants free rein to express their experiences, attitudes, and feelings. The following are some typical focus group questions:

- What experiences with your parish (diocese or faith community) have brought you closer to Jesus and to other members of your community?
- As you think about the future of your parish, what gives you hope and what gives you pause for concern?
- What are the ways in which the parish can be more engaging to youth and young adults?

LISTENING SESSIONS

Listening sessions or town hall meetings are opportunities to obtain input from entire communities at in-person sessions. Just like focus groups, listening sessions are not designed to achieve consensus or arrive at a conclusion, but rather to provide opportunity for people to express their reactions to proposed actions (draft pastoral or configuration plans) or their experiences, desires, and attitudes about special or generic subjects. Each listening session has an agenda, a timeframe, and a facilitator. Generally no session should last longer than ninety minutes.

If there is a draft document for reaction, it should be available to participants prior to the session. There should be a list of questions to be addressed during the session. The facilitator should work to make sure that a wide variety of people express their views. A recorder should record the input and produce a written record that should be freely available to any interested party. If the listening session is to generate information from a group about their attitudes and needs relative to their faith community, open-ended questions similar to those used in the focus groups can be used. The large number of people typically involved in a listening session, however, means that interaction among members of the group is limited so that all those interested can be heard.

If the purpose of the listening session is to obtain input to a draft statement of mission/vision, an entire pastoral plan, or a configuration plan, it is important to provide questions that focus on three issues: understanding, strengths, and opportunities for improvement. First, there should be an opportunity for participants to ask questions about the content of the document in order to achieve a fuller understanding of the content. Participants are then asked to focus on what is good, effective, and positive about the draft. Finally, participants are asked to focus on what could be improved in the draft. The answers to these questions provide important information to those doing the planning and enable them to craft a final statement that is easy to understand and is the best possible response to the issues. Listening sessions are just that. Members of the planning team should be present and can be invited to speak to answer checking or information questions. However, the facilitator should not allow the members of the planning team to engage in a debate with participants about the merits of the proposal. Members of the planning team need to reinforce with themselves that this is precisely a listening session.

SURVEYS

It is not unusual for participants in a planning process to suggest that a survey of parishioner attitudes or perspectives would be useful. They are almost always right. The problem is not that surveys are not useful. The problem is that they are difficult to construct, administer, and analyze. Unless a planning team has members with experience in this type of research, it should not attempt to gather information in this fashion. It will typically underestimate the time and effort involved, construct survey questions that do not provide valid and useful information, and fail to conduct sound statistical analysis. Often diocesan planning offices can provide this needed assistance or can recommend community resources that can. If the team does not include members competent in this type of research, local universities and research organizations do. Often these organizations can provide these services at low or no cost. The complete support program from Percept also provides these resources.

UNSOLICITED INPUT

While formal methods of listening are essential to an effective communication process, unsolicited input is also very valuable. If a person takes the initiative to send an email, write a letter, or make a phone call to express an opinion about planning, we can be sure that there are tens of people in the community who feel the same way. This type of input is easy to ignore, and it is important to give it its proper weight and not overvalue it, but it represents an important source of information. Sometimes this unsolicited input is verbal and comes to a planning team member second- or third-hand. This information is also valuable since it is part of the informal communication system within a community. However, it is also important to properly value and weigh that information and not be misled by the reverberation effect: one person expresses a perspective to a number of people, who repeat it to others, who repeat it to others. The result can appear to be a groundswell when in fact it is only the view of one or two people.

Communication Plan

KEY AUDIENCES

A communication plan has three elements: key audiences, key messages, and the media of transmission. This section will look at key audiences. It is tempting to think of the entire community as a homogeneous group with which the planning team needs to communicate. However, this is hardly ever the case. Any group is composed of sub-groups that differ in their base information, need for additional information, background and experience, future perspective, and engagement. The following is a list of the key audiences that are involved in almost any planning process:

- Faith community members (parishioners)
  - Present
  - Past but still involved
- Faith community staff
  - Pastoral
  - Support
- Formal lay leadership
- Informal lay leadership
- External community
- Leaders of other faith communities
  - Catholic

- Other
- Diocesan staff
- Bishop and Vicars General
- Often overlooked groups
  - Youth
  - Young adults
  - Seniors
  - Sick and infirm
  - Minority
    - Race
    - Sexual orientation
    - Immigration status

While long, this list is not exhaustive. In each local situation, it is important to view the community as composed of subgroups whose access to and experience with communication may be very different. For example, one would communicate in different ways to Spanish-speaking migrant members, majority teenagers, parish pastoral staff, and former parishioners. While the message would essentially be the same, the emphases and certainly the method of communication would differ. An effective communication plan begins with the identification of the key audiences.

KEY MESSAGES

Once the key audiences have been identified, the next step is to be clear about the messages to be communicated. Again, it is tempting to think that the message is a single message about everything that is happening, but this will lead to one massive communication, which is rarely the most effective method of transmitting information. The following list is a guide to thinking about the different types of information that can be part of a communication plan. Each of these has been discussed in previous chapters and will only be listed here as an aid to memory.

- Planning process
- Members of planning groups and teams
- Planning information
- Constraints and Church policies
- Reasons for planning
- Timelines
- Content: mission, vision, values, goals, objectives, action steps
- Overall process
- Frequently Asked Questions (FAQs)
- Bad news
- Information about other relevant situations
- Summary of feedback

The key messages for any specific planning setting will be idiosyncratic to that situation.

Frequently Asked Questions (FAQs) have proven to be particularly effective as part of a communication plan to support planning. This technique has been adapted from the technology arena (especially software) as a way to provide common and well-worked-out responses to the typical questions a user will have. Since lay leadership of a community does planning, and if the membership of a planning team is broadly representative of a community, it is relatively easy to construct the question part of FAQs. The questions are those that the members of the planning team themselves have. The problem is coming up with answers that are succinct, accurate, and stable. The time required to do this is well spent because it provides an efficient way to respond to most of the questions that most people will have. When the planning team encounters questions that are not in the FAQs, it needs to work out an answer and then add it to the list. Over time, a comprehensive list of FAQs is built that will be a powerful communication device in the local situation and will contribute to the work of other planning efforts as well.

MEDIA

The final piece of a communication plan is the media that will be used to communicate the key messages to the key audiences. Again these will vary by the specific planning situation, but the following is a suggested list.

- Homilies
- Bulletins
- Announcements at Mass
- Mailings
- Website
- Bulletin inserts
- Signs and posters
- Face-to-face individual or small-group meetings
- Large-group meetings
- Secular media
  - Press
  - Radio
  - Television
- Other

Faith community staff or volunteers can manage most of these methods of channels or communication. Use of the secular media may be off-putting to typical planning team members. If there are members who have experience dealing with the secular press, they should take the lead in managing that part of the communication process. If there are no such members, contact should be made with the communication office of the diocese for assistance and advice. Use of secular media is important because the larger community has an important stake in what happens to faith communities, but it may be unaware of the planning. Also, information that parishioners see in the secular media has greater credibility than the same information coming through channels that appear to be more subject to control by the Church.

Implementation

Implementation of a communication plan is the responsibility of a communication team formed as part of the overall planning process. This is a group of people whose major contribution is to make sure that key audiences receive the key messages in a timely fashion. As mentioned earlier, an effective communication process requires a dedicated communication team. If there are any communication professionals on the planning team, they should be recruited to provide leadership and support to this effort. The key to effectiveness is to build a communication plan and then persistently execute it.

A helpful tool for this implementation plan is a communication matrix organized by key messages. Thus for each key message, the communication team considers which media to use for each key audience as well as any adjustment in the tone or emphases of the message itself. The following is an example of such a planning matrix.

Communication Planning Sheet (Chart available at avemariapress.com)	
Key Message	Complete a planning sheet for each key message.
Key Audiences	Media and Timing
Parishioners Current	Describe the media and timing of communicating the key message for each key audience.
Parishioners Past	
Parish Pastoral Staff	
Parish Support Staff	
Lay Leadership	
External Community	
Leadership of Other Parishes	
Diocesan Staff	
Bishop	
Youth	
Young Adults	
Seniors	
Migrant Workers	

Conclusion

In this chapter we have reviewed the fundamentals of communication and its application to pastoral planning. Regardless of the level of planning (parish, regional, or diocesan), effective communication is essential to productive pastoral planning. The heart of the planning processes described in this book is the active engagement of the disciples of Christ in praying and thinking about the actions of the Body of Christ in a specific time and place. Given the hierarchical nature of the Church and the empowerment of the laity called for in Vatican II, planning can easily become dysfunctional unless relationships, processes, information, and objectives are clearly understood by all involved. This requires a commitment to systemic communication that would not have been necessary in a church in which clerics were to make decisions and lay people were to obey. Fortunately there is a body of knowledge and experience that can help the Church provide this kind of systemic communication.

We spent time understanding communication as the process by which information is exchanged between two or more people. We gained an appreciation for the complexity and interactivity of communication within an organization. We focused on eight rules of thumb for effective communication that we can use even if we cannot mount a comprehensive program as outlined here.

- During times of change, it is impossible to overcommunicate.
- Repetition is the heart of effective communication.
- Provide small bites rather than the whole steak.
- Opportunistic communication can support a formal communication process.
- Informal communication has a disproportionate impact on receivers.
- People are not at their best when they are surprised.

- The truth will set us free, even if the truth is troublesome.
- Feedback that makes a difference is crucial.

Before we focus on transmitting information to others, we need to understand the importance of listening to others. In fact, the secret of good communication is that it is based on listening just as much as active transmission of information. Good listeners not only hear more accurately what others are saying, but they also build an emotional bond with the other. We reviewed a set of techniques to help us be more effective listeners:

- Active listening
- Focus groups
- Listening sessions
- Surveys
- Unsolicited input

A comprehensive communication process is built on careful thinking about key audiences, key messages, and media. It is important to think about the various subgroups within our audience since people will communicate and receive information differently depending on their perspective and their peer groups. We also need to disaggregate messages so that we can tune communication more precisely, better understand the message in its complexity, and focus on communicating more digestible portions of information rather than everything at once. Finally, we need to look at the various media we have at our disposal for communicating with our intended audiences. All of this can be combined in a comprehensive communication matrix and plan. A special communication sub-team of the planning team is the best way to implement an effective communication effort.

Study Questions

1. How would you assess your ability and willingness to listen to others, especially those with whom you disagree or think you might disagree? What are the tactics you can implement to improve your listening behavior?
2. Which of the eight rules of thumb about communication makes the most sense to you and why? Which ones make the least sense and why? What rule(s) of thumb would you add to the list and why?
3. What are the advantages and the disadvantages of focus groups in pastoral planning?
4. How do you think your pastoral decision makers (pastor, bishop, lay leaders) do with regard to seeking and using input from those affected by decisions? How can they improve? Are you ever in a position in which you seek and use input? How well do you?
5. Thinking about your parish or faith community, how do the communication plan and its three elements (audience, message, media) make sense? Can you think of specific instances in which this approach would have improved overall functioning?

The following is a selected list of resources available in published form or online. **Additional material on Faith Sharing & Prayer and Group Processes is available for download at avemariapress.com.** The web resources noted below have existed for at least ten years and are maintained by well-established organizations.

PASTORAL COUNCILS

Fischer, Mark F. and Mary Margaret Raley, editors. *Four Ways to Building More Effective Pastoral Councils: A Pastoral Approach.* Mystic, CT: Twenty-Third Publications, 2002.
Written by highly regarded pastoral professionals with a wealth of experience, this is an effective overview of both pastoral councils and pastoral planning at the parish level.

Fischer, Mark F. *Pastoral Councils in Today's Catholic Parish.* Mystic, CT: Twenty-Third Publications, 2001.
Fischer is generally considered the expert on parish pastoral councils. He is a seminary faculty member and brings both personal experience and scholarship to this treatment of pastoral councils.

Gubish, Mary Ann, Susan Jenny, and Arlene McGannon. *Revisioning the Parish Pastoral Council: A Workbook.* Mahwah, NJ: Paulist Press, 2001.
This is the best book about parish pastoral councils. It is thoroughly informed by the principles of Vatican II, takes the spirituality of pastoral councils seriously, and focuses on practical and tested ways of establishing or re-establishing a pastoral council. While it deals only with parish pastoral councils, its basic message and insights can be easily applied to diocesan and regional councils.

PASTORAL PLANNING

Conference for Pastoral Planning and Council Development is the national organization for ministry professionals and lay leaders working in these fields. It has a comprehensive website (www.cppcd.org) that contains a great deal of information, including reports of research and development in pastoral planning and parish configuration.

Cork, Ron. *Making Your Pastoral Council Work: A Planning Guide for Parishes.* Ottawa: Novalis, 2007.
This is a pragmatic handbook for pastoral councils and their work of pastoral planning, written by the leading practitioner in the Canadian Church.

Rexhausen, Jeff, with Michael Cieslak, Mary L. Gauthier, and Robert J. Miller.

A National Study of Recent Diocesan Efforts at Parish Reorganization in the United States: Pathways for the Church of the 21ˢᵗ Century. Dubuque: Loras College Press, 2004.

This is the most recent national study of parish reorganization, and it provides important insights into effective processes that result in successful planning. This is an important resource for anyone seeking to understand how to design planning systems. It is available from the Council for Pastoral Planning and Council Development.

DEMOGRAPHICS

Percept is the only U.S. firm that provides demographic support for church planning. Users can access Percept directly through the website: www.perceptgroup.com. However, the most powerful and cost-effective method of using this resource is based on diocesan membership that provides effectively unlimited access to individual parishes through www.link2lead.com.

The U.S. Census Bureau (www.census.gov) provides a wide variety of demographic information free of charge. Since the U.S. census, unlike the Canadian census, does not ask any questions about religious affiliation, this information has limited utility in coming to understand religious behavior and needs. However, the basic socio-economic information, down to census track level and beyond, is available in a very user-friendly manner on the American FactFinder site: factfinder.census.gov.

There are often many additional demographic services available at the local level. These are typically associated with local universities, school districts, or local governments.

CHURCH STATISTICS

The Center for Advanced Research in the Apostolate (cara.georgetown.edu) at Georgetown University is the leading source of authoritative information on the Church in the United States. CARA tracks important information annually, produces special reports on a wide variety of important topics, and provides extensive services to support planning at the diocesan and parish level, especially survey research.

The Official Catholic Directory™ has been published annually since 1817. This is a comprehensive report on every U.S. diocese and includes listings of diocesan offices and personnel, all parishes and their personnel, and priests' assignments. Each diocese submits an annual report on a variety of administrative and sacramental information. Published by P. J. Kenedy & Sons, the often-named "Kenedy Directory" is generally considered the authoritative source of diocesan information. More information can be found on its website: www.catholicdir.com.

Clark, Bishop Matthew H. "Centrality of Eucharist: From East to West a Perfect Offering," Pastoral Letter on the Eucharist. October 24, 1996. Available online at: www.dor.org/planning/Resources/bishopclark.

Flannery, O.P., Austin, General Editor. *Vatican Council II: The Conciliar and Post Conciliar Documents.* Vol. I. Northport, NY: Costello Publishing, 2004.

This volume contains all the conciliar documents of Vatican II, including the ones most relevant to pastoral planning: *Lumen Gentium* (Dogmatic Constitution on the Church) and *Gaudium et Spes* (Pastoral Constitution on the Church in the Modern World).

McKenna, Kevin. *The Ministry of Law in the Church Today.* South Bend, IN: University of Notre Dame Press, 1999.

This is an excellent guide to contemporary canon law written for all members of the Church but especially for those without training in canon law. It is the best overall view of the purpose and nature of canon law in the contemporary Church. The same author has also written *A Concise Guide to Your Rights in the Catholic Church,* published by Ave Maria Press in 2006.

Pope John Paul II. *Novo Millennio Ineunte.* 2001.

This apostolic letter of John Paul II is the papal document that speaks most directly to the need for pastoral planning as the Church enters a new age.

Prusak, Bernard P. *The Church Unfinished: Ecclesiology Through the Centuries.* Mahwah, NJ: Paulist Press, 2004.

This is a comprehensive look at the Church from the beginning through the implementation of the teaching of Vatican II in *Gaudium et Spes* and *Lumen Gentium.* It is very helpful for an understanding of how the Church came to be organized as it is and the ways in which Vatican II sought to reclaim the fullness of the traditional teaching of the Church as both hierarchy and the People of God.

Rivers, Robert S. *From Maintenance to Mission: Evangelization and the Revitalization of the Parish.* Mahwah, NJ: Paulist Press, 2005.

This excellent book sets a stark choice before us. Are we to just take care of what we have in terms of people, buildings, organizations, and belief? Or are we to respond to Christ's commission to spread the Good News? If we think the second, then we must be prepared for change as we stretch beyond just maintaining what we have.

Sofield, Loughlan, and Carroll Juliano. *Collaboration: Uniting Our Gifts in Ministry.* South Bend, IN: Ave Maria Press, 2000.

This is a theologically sound and practical guide to what constitutes collaboration and how it can become part of the everyday reality in parishes and faith communities. It is a well-organized and readable treatment of a topic that is often advocated but rarely understood.

Archbishop Romero Prayer. The following is a prayer often used in pastoral planning. It is typically attributed to Archbishop Oscar Romero, assassinated in El Salvador in 1980. It appears, however, that the prayer was actually written by Bishop Kenneth Untener for delivery by Joseph Cardinal Dearden at a Mass for deceased priests. The text of the prayer below and the background is taken from a homily given by Bishop Thomas Gumbleton on March 28, 2004 and printed online by the *National Catholic Reporter*: www.nationalcatholicreporter.org

It helps now and then to step back and take the long view.

The Reign of God is not only beyond our efforts. It is beyond our vision.

We accomplish in our lifetime only a tiny fraction of the magnificent enterprise that is God's work.

Nothing we do is complete, which is another way of saying the Reign of God always lies beyond us.

No statement says all that could be said.

No prayer fully expresses our faith.

No confession brings perfection.

No pastoral visit brings wholeness.

No program accomplishes the church's mission.

We cannot do everything, but there is a sense of liberation in realizing that because this enables us to do something and to do it well.

It may be incomplete but it is a beginning, a step along the way, and an opportunity for God's grace to enter and do the rest.

Harter, SJ, Michael, editor. *Hearts on Fire: Praying with Jesuits.* St. Louis: Institute of Jesuit Sources, 1993.
A collection of prayers by St. Ignatius and the members of the Society of Jesus he founded. There are many familiar prayers, some of which are paraphrased to make them more accessible to our ears.

The Diocese of Rochester, New York, has extensive prayer and faith resources available on its pastoral planning website: www.dor.org/planning. Once on this page, the prayer and faith sharing resources, along with many others, can be found under the Planning Resources link. Also on this site are prayer and faith sharing resources provided by the Diocese of Albany. These provide a total of thirty-four faith sharing sheets along with instructions and helpful suggestions.

McCorry, Richard. *Dancing With Change: A Spiritual Response To Changes In The Church.* iUniverse: 2004.

This is a practical and theologically sound guide for individuals and faith communities confronting change. The author is establishing himself as an important resource for individuals, communities, and dioceses dealing with change—often not of their own making—by helping them deepen their spiritual and prayer life.

LEADERSHIP

Clark, Bishop Matthew H. "The Pastoral Exercise of Authority," *New Theology Review* (Aug. 1997).

Matthew Clark has been bishop of Rochester, New York, since 1979. This article is a brief but excellent review of how pastoral authority is to be exercised in a post-Vatican II Church. www.dor.org/planning/Resources/bishopclark.

Blanchard, Ken, and Eunice Parisi-Carew. *One Minute Manager Builds High Performing Teams*. Rev. ed. New York: William Morrow, 2000.

This is an excellent and succinct treatment of the leadership styles that match the development of any group. It provides easy-to-understand advice on how to diagnose the motivation and capacity of teams with regard to specific tasks and how to select the leadership styles that will move the team toward high performance. This is based on Blanchard's *One Minute Manager* and *Leadership and the One Minute Manager: Increasing Effectiveness through Situational Leadership*, both available from William Morrow.

Heifetz, Ronald. *Leadership Without Easy Answers*. Cambridge, MA: Belknap Press, 1998.

This is an excellent resource for those working with members of planning teams and pastoral councils. It is especially important for the insights it provides for those in leadership positions with high expectations, but with little real or perceived authority.

Smith, M. K. (2001) "Chris Argyris: Theories of Action, Double-loop Learning and Organizational Learning," *The Encyclopedia of Informal Education*, www.infed.org/thinkers/argyris.htm.

This is an excellent summary of the thought and work of Chris Argyris. It contains especially lucid descriptions of double- and single-loop learning.

Sofield, Loughlan, and Donald H. Kuhn. *The Collaborative Leader: Listening to the Wisdom of God's People*. South Bend, IN: Ave Maria Press, 1995.

The authors take an inductive approach to the understanding of leadership and its role in the lives of God's people. The analysis of the leadership of Jesus is especially well done and can provide a model for thinking about truly Christian leadership.

DIOCESAN PLANNING WEBSITES

Some of the best resources are those available on diocesan websites. These are designed to support planning efforts in specific dioceses and are typically updated with general information as well as examples of planning and planning documents from parishes, regional groups, and dioceses.

Diocese of Rochester, New York: www.dor.org/planning

Diocese of Greensburg, Pennsylvania: www.catholicgbg.org/DOGWeb/ wsotft3.nsf/SearchByKey/ A29F7951CC92FF7A85256B95006C04E3.html

Archdiocese of Philadelphia: www.archdiocese-phl.org/pastplan/

Diocese of Cleveland, Vibrant Parish Life Program: www.dioceseofcleveland.org/vibrantparishlife/

Archdiocese of Los Angeles: www.la-archdiocese.org/synod/ index.php

Diocese of Green Bay: www.gbdioc.org/

Archdiocese of Dubuque: www.arch.pvt.k12.ia.us/PastoralP/ pphome.html

PRACTICAL RESOURCES

Catholic Encyclopedia. Available online at www.newadvent.org/cathen/ index.html

This is an excellent starting point for research about the Church and its history.

Doyle, Michael. *How to Make Meetings Work.* New York: Jove, 1986.

This is the tried and true classic. It covers the basics for effective meetings.

Rumsey, Deborah. *Statistics for Dummies.* Hoboken, New Jersey: For Dummies, 2003.

This is an easy-to-understand and -use guide for creating and using statistics.

APPENDIX B: GLOSSARY

ACTION STEPS

Action steps are the specific tasks undertaken in any year to achieve an objective that in turn achieves a goal.

CODE OF CANON LAW

The systematic arrangement of the universal laws of the Roman Catholic Church that includes the structure and authority of the Church as well as the rights and responsibilities of members. There was a major revision of canon law in 1983 that incorporated the work of the Second Vatican Council.

CONFIGURATION PLANNING

This term is generally understood as the planning that deals with the number, location, and relationship of Catholic parishes. In many dioceses, configuration planning deals with the closing or merging of parishes in response to decline in Catholic population, relocation of Catholics out of the core areas of major cities into the suburbs, and the declining number of priests. Generally, configuration issues need to be dealt with before parishes can engage in effective pastoral planning for ministries at the regional level.

DEACON

Vatican II restored one of the earliest ministries in the Church, the diaconate, as a permanent office. Deacons assist priests with Eucharistic liturgies but cannot themselves preside. Deacons proclaim the Gospel and preach as part of their ministry in the Church. They often focus on the social ministry of parishes as well as assist with the preparation for and celebration of baptism and matrimony.

DEANERY

Deaneries are geographic regions of a diocese set up to facilitate certain ecclesial oversight. A dean is appointed by the diocesan bishop to oversee a deanery. In some dioceses, a vicariate and a vicar forane or a region and regional coordinator are used for the same purpose. The geographic size and composition of these regions varies among dioceses, but generally these include too many parishes to serve as effective planning groups. Generally there are no pastoral councils associated with these deaneries, vicariates, or regions.

DIOCESAN FINANCE COUNCIL

The finance council that advises the diocesan bishop. See "Finance Council" for a description.

DIOCESAN PASTORAL COUNCIL

The pastoral council that advises the diocesan bishop. See "Pastoral Council" for a description.

DIOCESAN SYNOD

A group of selected priests and other members of the Christian faithful of a particular Church that offers assistance to the diocesan bishop for the good of the entire diocesan community A bishop may call a diocesan synod in order to hear the broad membership of the diocesan church on matters of pastoral concern. Synods typically take three years from the beginning of preparation to the final celebration of the synod itself. Broad consultation throughout the parishes and other faith communities results in pastoral concerns coming before the entire diocesan church. The time and resources required for a successful synod are substantial, and thus synods are not regular events for dioceses.

DIOCESE

This is the "local church." A diocese is a portion of the people of God that is entrusted for pastoral care to a bishop, the community of disciples of Jesus Christ in a specific geographic area. Bishops exercise authority and responsibility in a specific local church to which they have been appointed by the Pope. In the United States, dioceses follow civil geographic boundaries (counties, for example) and are ordinarily named for the city in which the bishop presides in the diocesan cathedral.

DOUBLE-LOOP LEARNING

Chris Argyris and David Schön identify double-loop learning as the learning required when the ordinary rules and procedures do not seem to work. Rather than simply needing to find new rules, they argue we need to go back to the underlying values and goals to understand these in the new circumstances and thus create new rules and procedures. This is called double-loop learning because we must go deeper than the simple application of standard operating procedures (single-loop learning).

FINANCE COUNCIL

A group of the Christian faithful at the parish or diocesan level who assist the pastor or bishop by providing counsel in regards to financial matters, including assisting in the administration of temporal goods. The revised *Code of Canon Law* requires that each diocese (c. 492) and each parish (c. 537) have a finance council. Universal law as well as local diocesan legislation sets limits for significant financial and administrative decisions that require the bishop or pastor to consult with and receive the concurrence of the financial council. Each diocese should have available the local legislation pertaining to parish finance councils.

FOCUS GROUP

Developed as tools in market research, focus groups have been adapted to pastoral planning to elicit participants' reactions to pastoral issues and possibilities. These are free-flowing discussion groups led by an objective facilitator. The results, often including verbatim quotes, are provided to planners and decision makers to help them understand the desires and needs of church members.

GOALS

Goals are best next steps toward the future described in the vision statement. They are statements that describe future states that will move an organization toward its desired future. They describe what will be different in the ongoing behavior of an organization.

LAY ECCLESIAL MINISTER (LEM)

This term describes lay people who work as professionals in church ministries. LEMs typically have graduate degrees in theology and/or pastoral ministry. Their work covers a wide variety of positions, but typically they work in parishes and faith communities as Directors of Religious Education, Faith Formation, Social Ministry, Liturgy, and Music, to name a few. Many serve as pastoral ministers or pastoral associates participating with the pastoral leader in the direct pastoral care of faith community members. They also include Pastoral Administrators/Parish Life Coordinators or other titles of those who provide pastoral leadership to a faith community as authorized by a bishop under c. 217.2.

LAY MINISTRY LEADERS

Lay persons participate in the ministries of a parish or faith community in various ways. Often a lay member, sometimes assisted by a member of the pastoral staff, provides the leadership for a ministry. Such ministries could include chairs of social ministry, liturgy, or stewardship committees.

LAY PERSON

A lay person is a member of the Christian faithful who is not ordained (bishop, priest, deacon). (Technically, religious men and women who are not ordained are considered members of the laity.)

LISTENING SESSION

Listening sessions are opportunities to obtain input from entire communities via in-person contact. They are not designed to achieve consensus or arrive at a conclusion but rather to provide opportunity for people to express their reactions to proposed actions, or their experiences, desires, and attitudes about special or generic subjects.

MISSION

A mission is a task given by one person to another. In the case of the Church, each baptized member is given the mission of Jesus Christ: announce the Reign of God to all, especially those forgotten by society, and do works of justice and mercy.

MISSION STATEMENT

A mission statement is a formal expression of the reason for being of an organization or community. It describes the work of the organization and why the organization and its work matters.

OBJECTIVES

Objectives are activities, typically extending over a multi-year time period, that are required to achieve the goals of a plan. They have definite time frames, expected results, and defined responsibility.

OPPORTUNITY COST

Opportunity cost measures the cost of a proposed action by describing the actions that will not be possible because this one is chosen. It is a way of measuring the relative value of options competing for our time and resources.

PARISH

A parish is "a definite community of Christian faithful established on a stable basis within a diocese" (see c. 515 §1). Typically, though not always, a parish has geographic boundaries. The pastor or pastoral leader is responsible for the pastoral care of all those within the parish boundaries.

PARISH CLUSTER

This is a rather imprecise term. It generally refers to a situation in which a pastor or pastoral leader is assigned by the bishop to two or more parishes.

PARISH FINANCE COUNCIL

The finance council that assists a pastor or pastoral leader, see "Finance Council" for a definition.

PARISH LIFE COORDINATOR

One of the titles sometimes used by dioceses for someone other than a priest assigned by the bishop to be accountable to him for the pastoral care of a parish (see c. 517 §2). See also "Pastoral Administrator."

PARISH PASTORAL COUNCIL

This is a pastoral council that serves a parish. See "Pastoral Council" for a definition.

PASTORAL ADMINISTRATOR

One of the titles used by some dioceses for someone other than a priest assigned by the bishop to be accountable to him for the pastoral care of a parish (see c. 517, §2). See also "Parish Life Coordinator."

PASTORAL COUNCIL

A pastoral council is a group of the faithful, broadly representative of the faith community, who advise the pastoral leader on important pastoral issues. The proper work of a pastoral council is to identify and ponder pastoral issues and to recommend creative and effective responses. These recommendations are made to the pastor or pastoral leader at the parish level or to the bishop at the diocesan level. Canon law permits and encourages diocesan bishops to establish a diocesan pastoral council "to the extent that pastoral circumstances recommend it" (c. 511). Canon law also allows the diocesan bishop to require parish pastoral councils, after listening to his presbyteral council. Both diocesan and parish pastoral councils are consultative bodies without deliberative power to make decisions.

PASTORAL PLANNING

The process of praying and thinking together about the actions of the Body of Christ in a specific place and at a specific time. This can take place at the diocesan, regional or parish levels.

PASTORAL PLANNING CYCLE

This is an integrated process for a faith community to move through an ongoing process composed of mission, vision, goals, objectives, action steps, and evaluation.

PRESBYTERAL COUNCIL

Every diocesan bishop is required by canon law (c. 495) to have a presbyteral (priests') council. According to c. 495, it is "a body of priests who are to be like a senate of the bishop, representing" the priests of the diocese. "This council is to aid the bishop in the governance of the diocese . . . [so] that the pastoral welfare of the portion of the people of God entrusted to [the bishop] may be promoted as effectively as possible." Since the bishop is required by c. 515 §2 to listen to the presbyteral council before "notably altering" a parish, the bishop will typically take the results of pastoral plans that materially impact the life of a parish or group of parishes to the presbyteral council for consultation before he makes a final decision about the plan.

PRIESTS' COUNCIL

See "Presbyteral Council."

STEWARDSHIP

Stewardship is a profound recognition of our giftedness by God and an overwhelming sense of gratitude. We are blessed with gifts in order to place them at the service of others.

TEMPORALITIES

The material goods owned, cared for, and administered by the Church at all levels. These include, for example, real property, buildings, technology infrastructure, financial investments, and other assets. In short, these are earthly goods, which the Church has a right and need to own in order to pursue its spiritual mission in the world.

VATICAN II

The Second Vatican Council was called by Pope John XXIII as an ecumenical council, that is, one to which all bishops were called along with observers from other Christian churches and non-Christian religions. It met from 1962 to 1965. It was called by the Pope to renew and update the Church. Two documents— Dogmatic Constitution on the Church (*Lumen Gentium*) and the Pastoral Constitution on the Church in the Modern World (*Gaudium et Spes*)—are particularly important for pastoral planning.

VICARIATES

See "Deanery."

VISION STATEMENT

A vision statement describes where an organization sees itself in the future. It is a word picture of a future state in which either key problems are resolved or in which ideals are more fully realized or both. It is typically written in the present tense as though it had already been realized. This helps the reader experience the look and feel of what the world would be like if the mission of an organization were more fully realized.

William L. Pickett served as the Director of Pastoral Planning for the Diocese of Rochester, New York, from 1997 to 2006. That role strengthened his spiritual life and led him to a deeper understanding of what it means to be a church. He has thirty years of experience in higher education administration and served as the president of St. John Fisher College in Rochester for ten years.

Pickett, who holds a Ph.D. in higher education from the University of Denver, is currently pursuing an M.A. in theological studies from St. Bernard's School of Theology and Ministry. He remains an active presenter and consultant in the field of organizational planning, with particular expertise in pastoral planning. Pickett lives in Rochester with his wife Marilyn. This is his first book.

Series editor Fr. Kevin E. McKenna is the pastor of St. Cecilia Parish in Rochester, New York. He has served as chancellor of the Diocese of Rochester, New York and president of the Canon Law Society of America. Fr. McKenna is the author of numerous books and articles on Church law and ministry.

THE CONCISE GUIDE SERIES

The Concise Guide Series, edited by Kevin McKenna, tackles questions of central importance for contemporary Catholicism. Each book in the series carefully outlines the issues, references the necessary documents, and sketches answers to pressing pastoral questions.

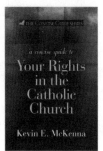

A Concise Guide to Your Rights in the Catholic Church

Decodes complex Roman Catholic Church law and doctrine into a practical, sound reference book. It familiarizes Catholics with the rights and obligations written into Church law for all its members while outlining the procedures in place for vindicating these rights. .
ISBN: 9781594710798 / 128 pages / $12.95

A Concise Guide to Canon Law
A Practical Handbook for Pastoral Ministers

This handy reference provides a compact overview of the most important canonical issues facing pastoral ministers. Arranged by topic, it offers a thorough summary of Church law and is complete with reference numbers to relevant canons in the Code of Canon Law. Helpful "frequently asked questions and answers" make finding answers to the most often-asked questions even easier.
ISBN: 9780877939344 / 128 pages / $10.95

A Concise Guide to Catholic Social Teaching

A welcome distillation of social principles presented in both papal encyclicals and pastoral letters developed by the American bishops. Includes reflection questions ideal for individual or group usage and an appendix that offers an extensive homily guide and sample penance service.
ISBN: 9780877939795 / 160 pages / $12.95

TOGETHER in MINISTRY
ave maria press®

ave maria press
Notre Dame, IN 46556
www.avemariapress.com • Ph: 800-282-1865
A Ministry of the Indiana Province of Holy Cross
Available from your local bookstore or from ave maria press

Keycode: FØAØ8Ø7ØØØØ